Silk Arrangements

by Mary Gudgeon and John Clowes

Silk Arrangements

MARY GUDGEON
& JOHN CLOWES

M & J PUBLICATIONS

Contents

Introduction 5

Before you start
Material and mechanics 6
Bases and containers 8
The flowers for arranging 10
Foliage and accessories 12
The technique of wiring 14
Candles and their preparation 16
Ribbons and their tying 18
The shapes to follow 20

Step-by-step arrangements
Lotus Eaters 22
Apricot and Cream 24
Silk Curves 26
Iris & Pussy Willow 28
Peach Delight 30
Ruby Woodslice 32
Tropical Dish 34
Pink Crescent 36
Summer Sun 38
Pink Sensation 40
Spring Profusion 42
Poppy Fields 44
Days of Spring 46
Bowl of Plants 48
Chelsea Boot 50
Handful of Freesias 52
Basket of Blue 54
Trails of Fuchsia 56
Daisy Basket 58
Riverside Tulips 60
Gardenia Cage 62
Golden Lightness 64
Alabaster Smoothness 66
Sweet Peas 68
Pink Roses 70
After Eight Candelabra 72
Mauve Slice 74
Green Sleeves 76
Blossom Tree 78
Summer Splendour 80
Lemon Candle 82
Childs Play 84
Carnation Centrepiece 86
Copper Cocktail 88
Waterside Blossom 90
Orange Glow 92

Final touches
Finishing Off 94
Index 96

First published in Great Britain in 1985 by M & J Publications, The Hollies, Cattlegate Road, Crews Hill, Enfield, Middx, England EN2 9DW.

ISBN 0 9509748 1 1

Arrangements by Mary Gudgeon, John Clowes, Mark Clowes and Nicholas Clowes.

Production Services by Book Production Consultants, Cambridge.
Printed in Great Britain by Blantyre Printing & Binding Co Ltd, Glasgow.
Photography by Carleton Photographic Services Ltd (0992) 27866.
Artwork and design by Goldcrest Design (Fleet 29657).

Introduction

Artificial flowers have come a long way since the first plastic daffodil. Nowadays there is a host of 'silk' material available of such superb quality that only its permanence gives away the secret that the stems are not real.

With this colourful and exciting book anyone can introduce the beauty of 'silk' flower arrangements into their home. Whether you are an experienced arranger or just a beginner you will find shapes, designs and colour ideas which should inspire you into action.

There is nothing complicated to learn and you don't have to be gifted with an artist's eye to re-create the arrangements which form the core of this book. We have listed the material we have used and have provided step-by-step instructions on how each arrangement was made. Simple line drawings illustrate the starting points. On separate pages you will find detailed instructions and diagrams on how to wire individual flowers, lengthen stems and tie ribbons. It couldn't be easier or more satisfying.

Unlike arranging fresh flowers there is nothing to fear and mistakes don't matter a jot. If things go wrong you can dismantle your creation and start again. Your flowers are everlasting and can be used in several different arrangements. The beauty they provide will be a joy for years rather than days, so have a go. You *can* do it too!

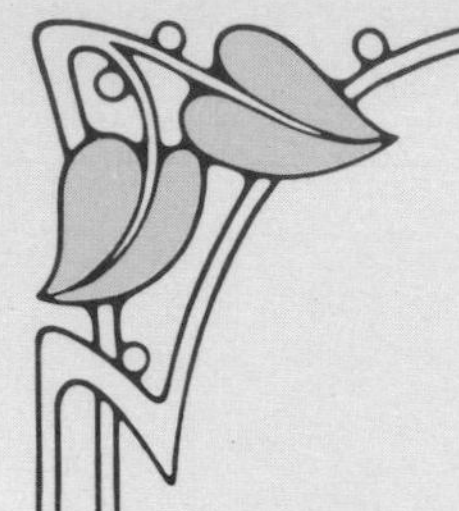

The materials available

You don't need a mountain of equipment to make flower arrangements with artificial material, but some things like an efficient pair of wire cutters will make life easier.

1. **Wire Cutters**
   You can use a pair of pliers borrowed from the tool kit or buy a handy pair of wire cutters specially produced for florist work. You will need them to cut stems to length as well as to trim wires evenly. Florist scissors often have a special notch which is suitable for cutting thin wire.

2. **Wire**
   Stub wires are useful for adding stems to flowers and foliage pieces. They are available in various lengths and thicknesses. A small packet of two different gauges will be enough to start with.

Useful Extras

3. Scissors for trimming foliage and cutting ribbon.

4. A knife for cutting blocks of Oasis and curling ribbon.

5. Stemwrap for covering the wire stems of material to give a natural green colour. This is also available in brown and white.

The mechanics you will find useful

The word 'mechanics' is used in flower arranging circles to describe the devices which are used to hold flower and foliage stems in position.

The pieces of green plastic foam which absorb water and are used as a base for fresh flowers are well known. However, the brown plastic foam pieces and the various types of clay material used for dried and artificial material may be new to you. Your local garden centre will be sure to have some of them available.

6. **Oasis tape**
   One side of the tape is adhesive and is used to stick over the foam block and onto the container if the arrangement is very large and thick stems are used such as gladioli.

7. **Green Plastic Foam**
   If you are adding fresh flowers or foliage to an arrangement it is vital to use green plastic foam of Oasis for fresh flowers. Soak this in water thoroughly before use.

   Remember that wire stems inserted into this wet material will tend to go rusty. You can prevent this damage by simply varnishing the stems to waterproof them.

8. **Brown Plastic Foam**
   Various shapes are available in this material from block, to ball and cones.

9. **Plasticine or 'Stay Soft'**
   This type of material which will not set solid is essential when you are positioning candles which will need to be replaced after they have been burned.

10. **Dri-Hard**
    This material will set solid after about 12 hours and is useful to create a permanent arrangement. This material cannot be used again as it tends to crumble when the arrangement is dismantled.

11. **Plasticine Anchors**
    This tiny four-pronged anchor is used to hold the mechanics (foam block, plasticine or Dri-Hard) in a container so that they do not slip or fall over when you have completed the arrangement. One anchor is usually sufficient for most arrangements but more may be needed if you have a long sausage-shaped base or a large block to hold steady.

12. **Oasis Fix**
    A fixative material is needed to secure the plasticine anchor to the container of your choice. Oasis fix is a brand name for one of these fixatives but others are just as suitable.

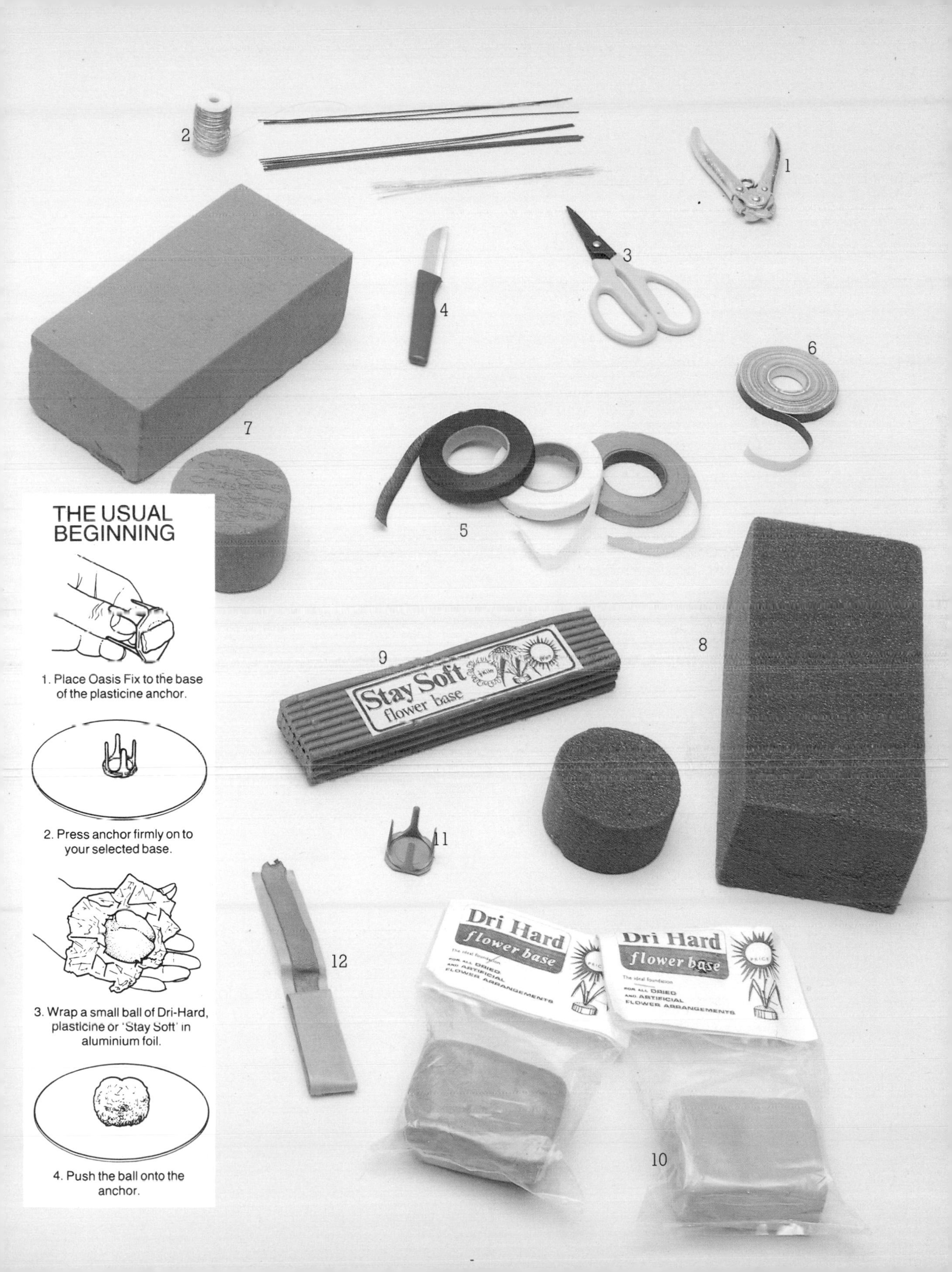

2
1
3
4
6
7
5
8
9
Stay Soft
flower base
11
12
Dri Hard
flower base
The ideal foundation
FOR ALL DRIED AND ARTIFICIAL FLOWER ARRANGEMENTS
Dri Hard
flower base
The ideal foundation
FOR ALL DRIED AND ARTIFICIAL FLOWER ARRANGEMENTS
10
THE USUAL BEGINNING
1. Place Oasis Fix to the base of the plasticine anchor.
2. Press anchor firmly on to your selected base.
3. Wrap a small ball of Dri-Hard, plasticine or 'Stay Soft' in aluminium foil.
4. Push the ball onto the anchor.

The bases you can find

In this book we have used simple bases and containers which you can buy easily and cheaply. Some you will already have around the house, some you will be able to improvise. If you own more elaborate containers by all means use them, remembering the balance between an arrangement and its container is important.

Wood Slices

These are available in various sizes which can be bought either with a polished surface or a rough one. Remember to check the underside for roughness before placing these bases on a polished surface.

Scroll Bases

Black is the most commonly found colour in various sizes.

Wicker Baskets

Various shapes and sizes are available which you should match with the size of flowers you plan to use. If you are using fresh material, line the basket with aluminium foil to prevent water damage.

Kitchen Dishes

Many of the lids from casseroles and heat proof dishes make admirable bases for arrangements.

The containers you can find

A small collection of the different types of containers will not cost you a fortune nor be difficult to find. You can use home-made lids instead of plastic saucers and painted plastic bottles instead of vases.

Saucers

White, black and beige saucers are available, some of which are designed to take the standard size plastic foam cylinder.

Candlesticks

Silver may be super, but plastic is cheaper. The only thing to consider is to make sure the base is large enough to keep it stable.

Candle Cups

These specially shaped cups fit into the top of a candlestick or wine bottle and have a large enough container to take a plastic foam cylinder or hold an amount of plasticine.

To ensure the candle cup sits firmly in the candlestick first wrap the base with Oasis fix or plasticine.

Wrought-iron Containers

These matt black containers are most useful for arranging artificial material. Some pedestal bases are adjustable so that the rod can be made tall or short.

The silk flowers for arranging

Most garden centres, florists and department stores will have available a vast array of silk flowers on display throughout the year. You can pay a few pence for a single rose or several pounds for a spray of blossoms.

The larger the stock the more variety of shades and colours you can find. When selecting the flowers of your choice consider separately each of the arrangements you are going to make. In this way you can compare and contrast the different shades available so that they match your decor or the end result you have in your mind's eye.

It is all a balancing act of finding the right flowers in the right colour and shade in the right size of bloom.

The natural flowering times of certain flowers are worth considering. Mixing tulips with chrysanthemums may not be the best choice as they rarely flower together.

It is also worth considering the display times for each arrangement. Some could be on show all year through but others, like spring daffodils and tulips, are best on display from January to May.

Here is a list of some flowers and foliage with the most appropriate display times.

Spring	**Summer**	**Autumn**	**Winter**
Daffodils	Roses	Chrysanthemums	Poinsettias
Tulips	Carnations	Asters	Christmas Roses
Anemones	Fuchsias	Daisies	Roses
Camellias	Geraniums	Roses	Carnations
Hyacinths	Delphiniums	Gladioli	Glixia
Snowdrops	Poppies	Dahlias	Holly
Lily-of-the-valley	Iris	Scabious	Mistletoe
Crocus	Lilies	Hebe	Pine

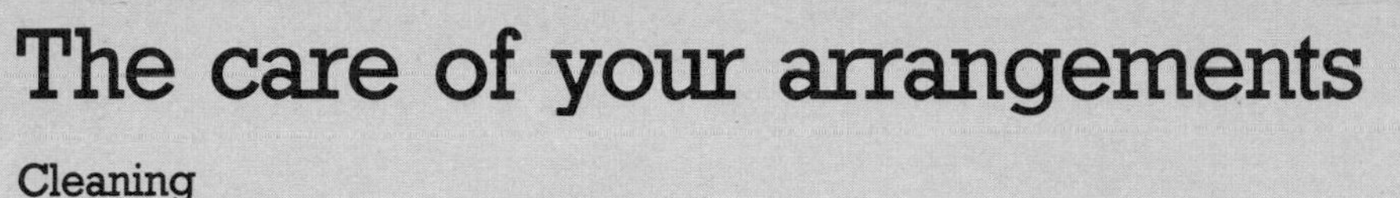

The care of your arrangements

Cleaning

Dust is the biggest problem with silk arrangements. Inevitably this grey layer will make your decorations look dead and dull.

Regular removal of dust will help to keep the flowers bright and fresh. You can simply blow off the settling dust occasionally or use your vacuum cleaner if you are specially careful.

Most people however prefer to wash their arrangements to remove the dust. Most 'silk' flowers are actually made from polyester material and are safely washable.

Find a bucket or bowl which is large enough to take all the stems of the arrangement. Almost fill the container with warm water and add a dash of washing-up liquid.

Now turn the arrangement upside down and immerse gently into the water making sure that the Dri-Hard or other holding material remains dry. Lift the arrangement in and out of the soapy water a few times to remove the dust. Replace the soapy water with fresh clean water and rinse the arrangements a couple of times, again making sure that the Dri-Hard does not get wet.

Storage

A complete arrangement can be stored without trouble in a plastic bag in a cupboard or in the loft. You may find it helpful to wash the arrangement before storage.

If you are dismantling an arrangement it is useful to store the flower stems in separate paper bags, one for each colour. In this way it will be easier to find the right shade you need in the future.

Foliage and accessories for arranging

Nowadays you should be able to find plenty of stems of different types of foliage to compliment the flowers you have chosen. Keep this foliage in scale and style with the arrangement you have in mind. That doesn't mean that the leaves should always blend in – you may find that a contrasting 'sharp' edge of spiky leaves is right for the shape you have in mind.

Also bear in mind the seasons and mix appropriate material. For example, catkins and pussy willow are very much for spring arrangements and while admirable for mixing with daffodils and iris they are not visually appropriate for chrysanthemums and sweet peas.

Some of the foliage used in the arrangements in this book is only available in large branches. Where this is so, we have cut this large branch down into smaller pieces and added a wire stem to each piece. (See page 15.) Usually one large branch has been sufficient for one arrangement.

Fresh Foliage

If you are tempted to use fresh, living foliage in an arrangement you must use the right type of Oasis foam as the base. Soak the foam in water and then push onto a plasticine anchor firmly fixed to the bottom of your container.

It is always advisable to stand fresh foliage in a bucket of water for several hours before you start arranging the material. This long drink will help to lengthen the life of the arrangement.

Try not to remove the stems and replace them in a different position too often. The foam for fresh material can soon disintegrate unlike the firm base used for artificial material.

The wire stems of the silk flowers which you use with fresh foliage can turn rusty after they have been kept wet for several days. To avoid this you should paint the base of the stems with varnish to protect the metal or use Stemwrap if the stem is just wire. Unwanted nail varnish is fine and so are the polyurethane-type wood sealants which are used for protecting doors or furniture.

Accessories

There are several items which can be included in an arrangement which add extra interest and different textures. Drift wood, moss, pebbles and fruit can all be used as accessories where appropriate to improve the shape or look of an arrangement.

Candles are an important part of dinner party arrangements. The soft glow of candle-light adds a touch of luxury to any gathering whether large or small. Remember to prepare the candle with cocktail sticks (details on page 17) and to use plasticine as the base so that the candles can be replaced easily.

There are other accessories which are placed below or to the other side of an arrangement to add atmosphere to the set piece. On page 23 we have used an oriental figure to amplify the tropical beauty of the lotus flowers.

You could use copper and brass objects, miniature tea cups, shells and even lids of casserole dishes to great effect.

The technique of wiring

With most artificial material you will frequently need to lengthen a stem or add a completely new one. Using florist wire and covering it with a green stem-binding tape is the easiest and firmest way. A wire stem allows the arranger to position the flower

HOW TO WIRE A FLOWER

1

Bend a stub wire in half and place the bend over the existing stem.

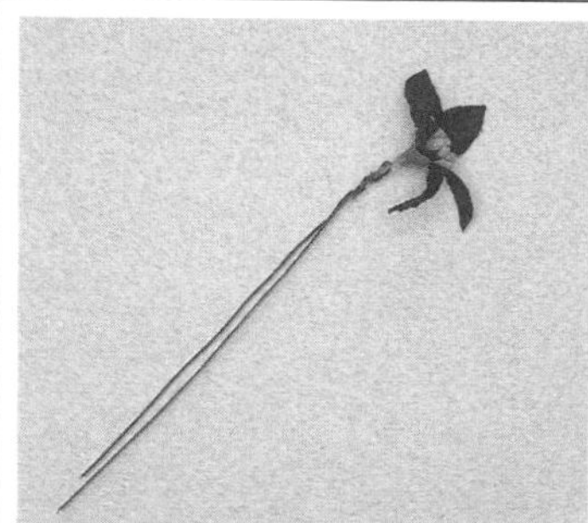

2

Twist one of the wire ends (called a 'leg') firmly around the stem and the other wire.

3

Use wire cutters to cut the ends to the required length.

4

Wrap wires with stem-binding tape.

HOW TO WIRE A LEAF

1

Work on the back of the leaf and stitch a wire through the centre of the leaf.

2

Bend both the wires down towards the base of the leaf.

3

Twist one wire 'leg' tightly around the stem and the other wire.

4

Wrap wires with stem-binding tape.

or leaf in exactly the right spot. Some wires are pictured on page 6.

Different thicknesses (gauges) of wire are available from very fine 'silver' reel wire to chunky, short stem wires. The general rule is to use the thinnest wire which is just sufficiently strong to do the job required. In this way your arrangement will not lose its natural look and become too rigid.

HOW TO WIRE A BRANCH

1

Place a wire across the stem.

2

Bend the stub wire in half.

3

Twist one of the wire ends (called a 'leg') firmly around the stem and the other wire.

4

Wrap wires with stem-binding tape.

HOW TO LENGTHEN A STEM

1

You can use the same method as wiring a branch shown on the left or the one illustrated here.

For oxtra long otomo oimply plaoo a wiro against the existing stem so that there is at least 2 inches of overlap.

2

Now start wrapping Stemwrap very tightly around the existing stem, gradually working over the join and down onto the new wire stem. It is important to keep the stemwrap tight at all times.

Candles

Candles have a vital role to play in dinner party arrangements. Even if not lit at the time they add a touch of luxury to the surroundings.

It is important that the candles are easily replaceable so that the line of the decoration is not ruined and new candles can be re-lit on another evening.

To achieve this, use plasticine or 'Stay-Soft' as your base material or use a block of plastic foam for artificial flowers. Prepare the candle with cocktail sticks before it is positioned in an arrangement. This technique means that the candle can be positioned more easily in a true vertical position.

There are many candles available nowadays of all shapes, sizes and colours. When selecting a candle for use in an arrangement, bear in mind that once lit the flame will gradually creep lower and lower. If you light the candle it must be extinguished before it reaches the flowers or foliage, especially if they are polyester or plastic. It is also worth considering that the thicker the candle the slower it will burn. It is wise therefore to choose the thickest candle possible which remains in proportion to the rest of the arrangement.

When positioning candles, make sure that they are straight and perfectly vertical from all angles. A slight tilt will become most irritating at a later date.

When you use several candles in an arrangement make sure that they are not all the same height – simply buy candles of different lengths. If you cannot find different sizes in the same colour then buy all of them in the tallest size and cut the others down with a knife.

Candlesticks

Creating a flower arrangement on the top of a candlestick is popular. Buy a special candle cup in a colour to match the base and fit into the candlestick using Oasis fix.

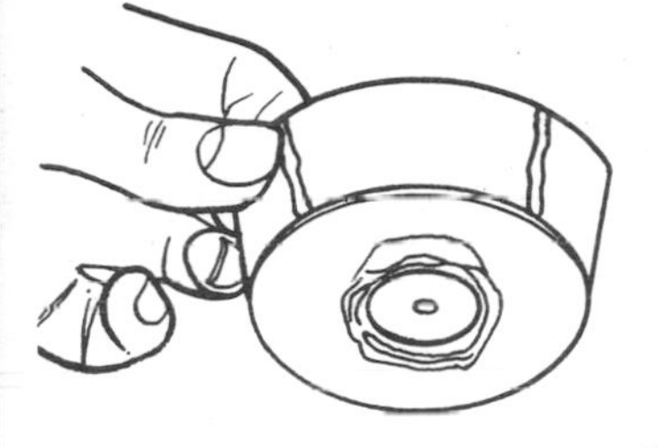

Wrap Oasis fix around the base of the cup.

Push firmly into the top of the candlestick.

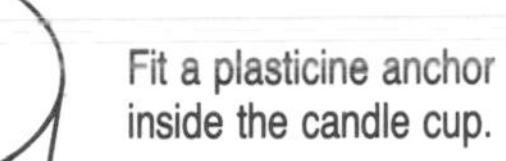

Fit a plasticine anchor inside the candle cup.

Push a circular piece of plastic foam into the cup or a ball of plasticine onto the anchor.

Preparing candles

Break two cocktail sticks in half and tape the four pieces to the base of the candle, making sure that the sticks which are to go into the foam are the same length.

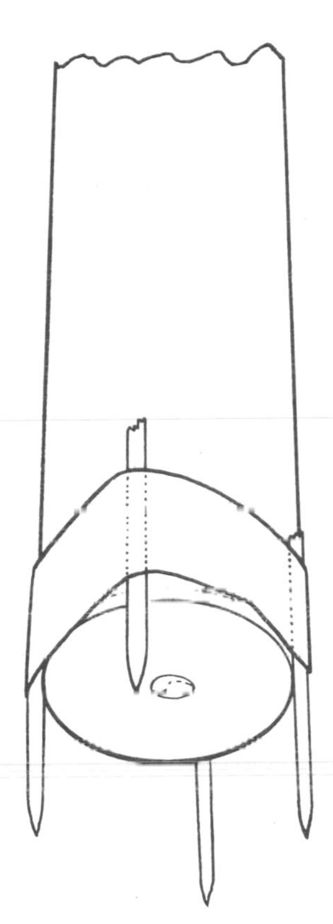

Candle Holders

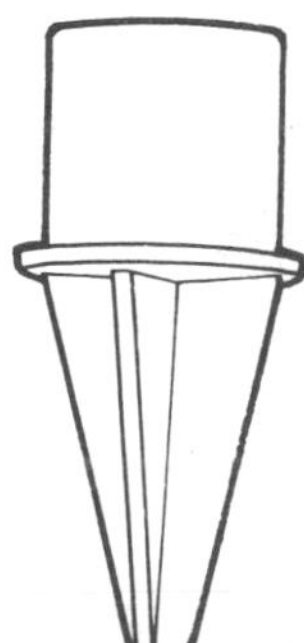

Small plastic holders are available for a few pence which hold a candle firmly and push easily into plastic foam.

Tying Ribbons

Many people find that tying ribbons and bows to make them look pretty is a difficult job. However with a little practice and the following step-by-step instructions everyone should be able to add a crisp bow to their arrangements without trouble.

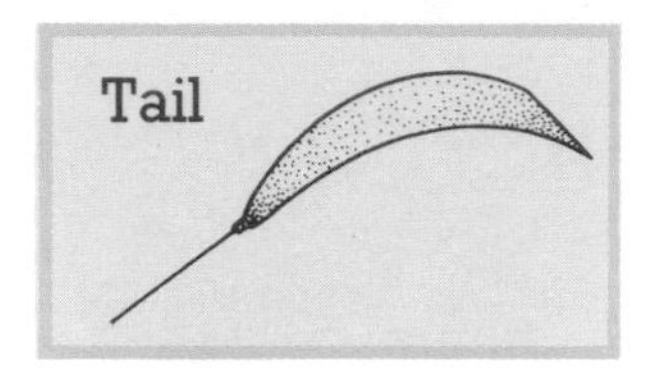

This ribbon piece is simply a length of ribbon which has been pinched together at one end with a double leg wire added.

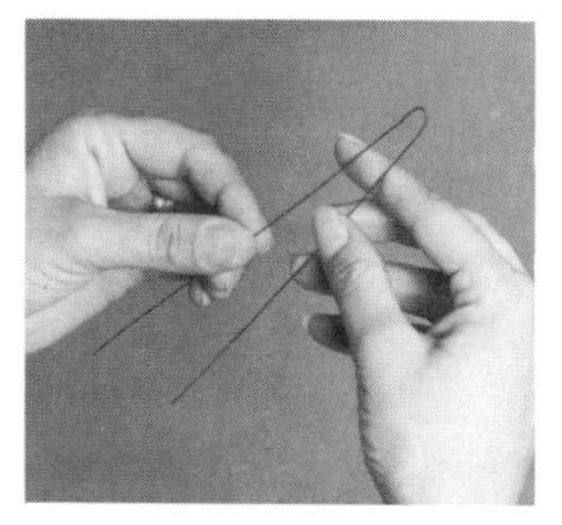

1. Bend a stub wire in half.

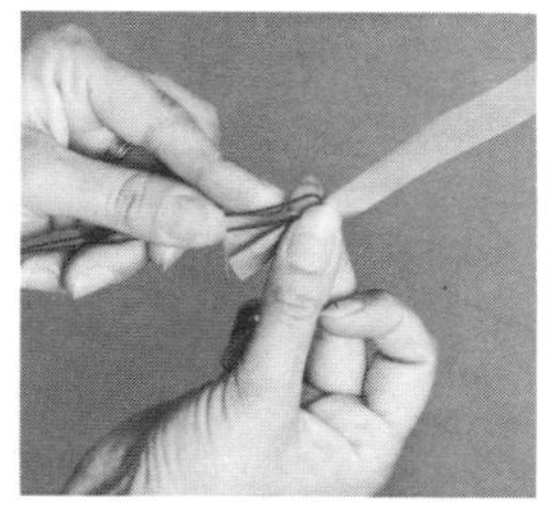

2. Pinch the end 1 inch of ribbon together and place the bend of wire onto the ribbon.

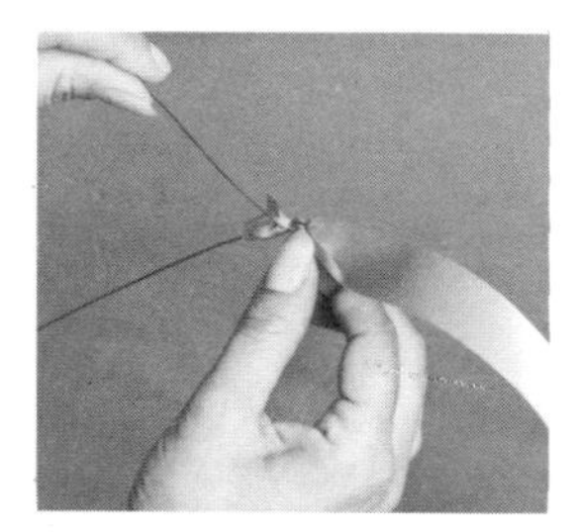

3. Twist one wire leg around the ribbon and the other wire to firmly trap the ribbon and produce a sturdy stem.

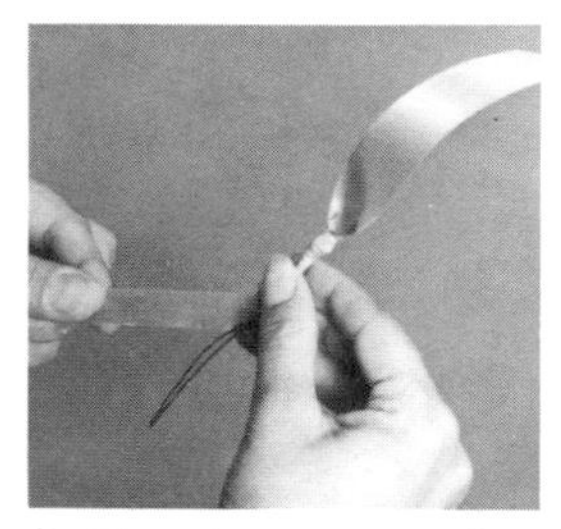

4. Use wire cutters to trim ends evenly. Wrap wires with stem-binding tape.

This is the most versatile of ribbon pieces. It can be used singly or can be positioned with stems pointing towards each other to give the impression of a figure of eight bow.

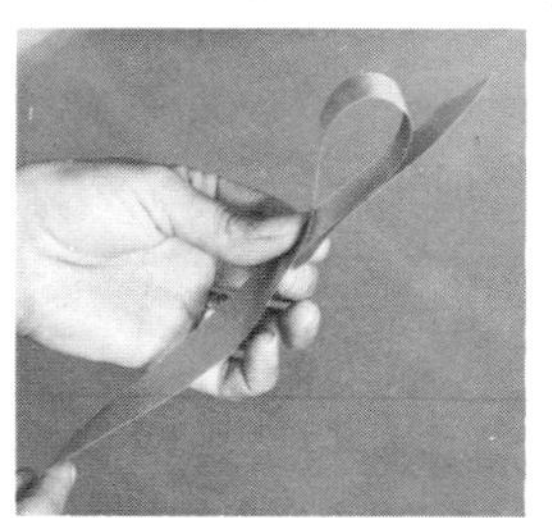

1. Hold the ribbon to make one loop and a tail to the required length.

2. Pinch the end of the loop firmly together and hold. Then cut the remaining ribbon from the roll.

3. Bend a stub wire in half and place the bend over the pinched end of the ribbon.

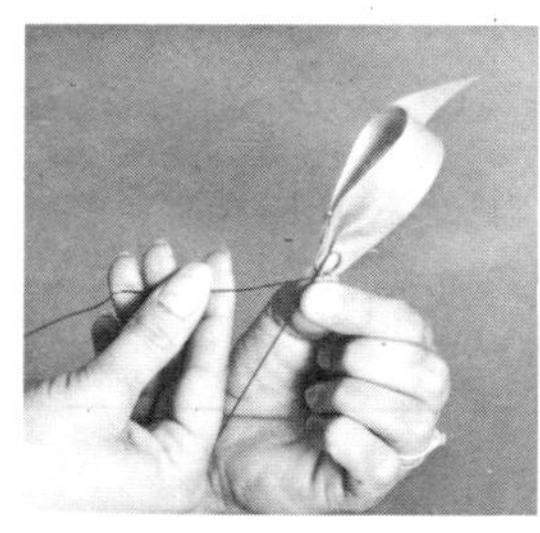

4. Twist as tightly as possible and wire leg around the pinched part of the ribbon and the other length of wire.

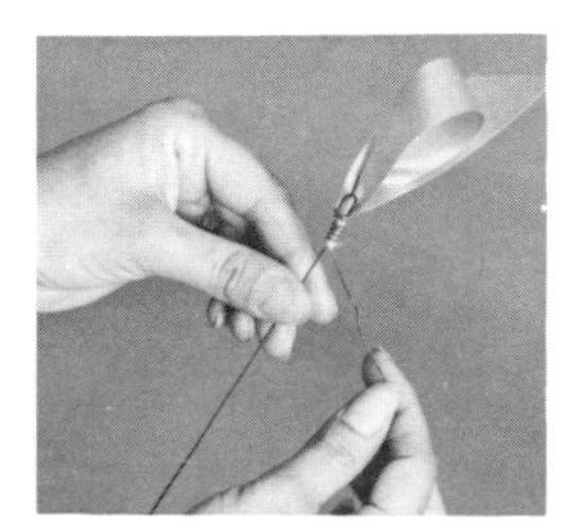

5. Twist several times to trap the ribbon and produce a sturdy stem.

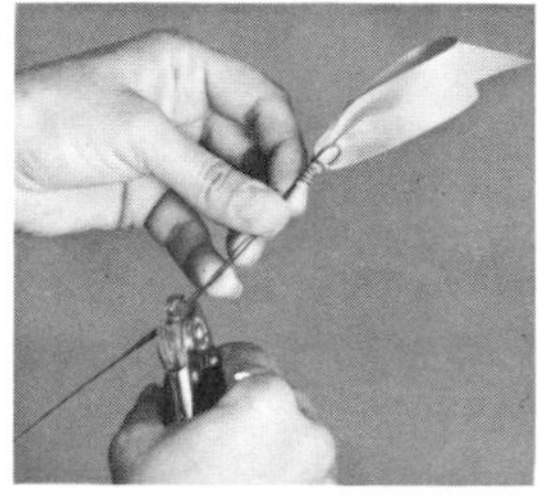

6. Cut wires to required length.

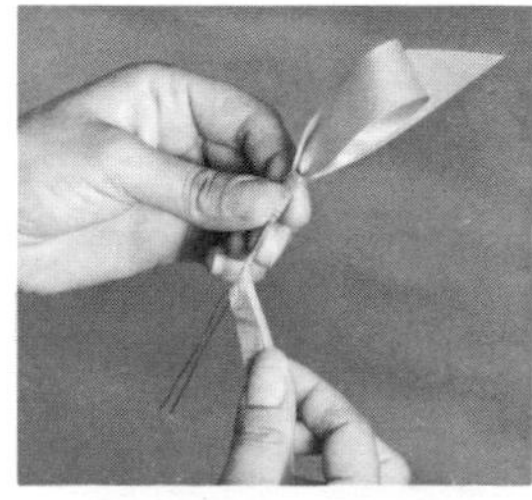

7. Wrap wires with stem-binding tape.

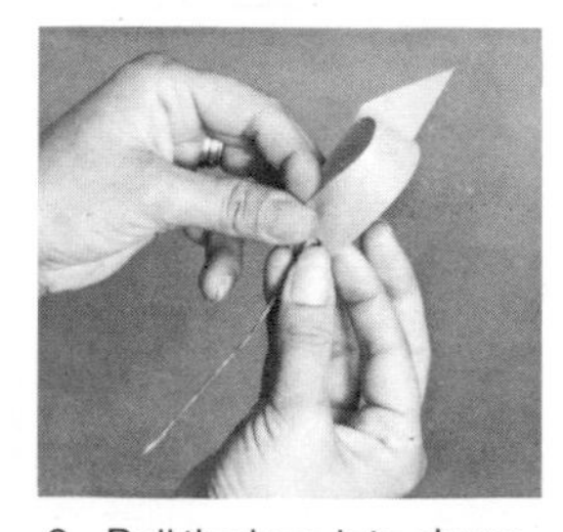

8. Pull the loop into shape.

A useful ribbon piece for the experienced arranger.

1. Hold the ribbon to make two loops and a tail to the required length.
2. Follow steps 2-8 as shown in the Single Loop instructions.

For bigger and bold arrangements this larger bow is most useful.

1. Hold the ribbon to make three loops and a tail to the required length.
2. Follow steps 2-8 as shown in the Single Loop instructions.

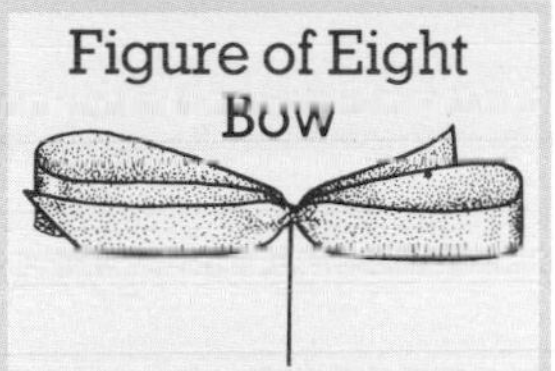

Illustrated below is the easiest way for the inexperienced to tie a figure of eight bow. A professional will pinch the ribbon together at each stage, but this needs practice.

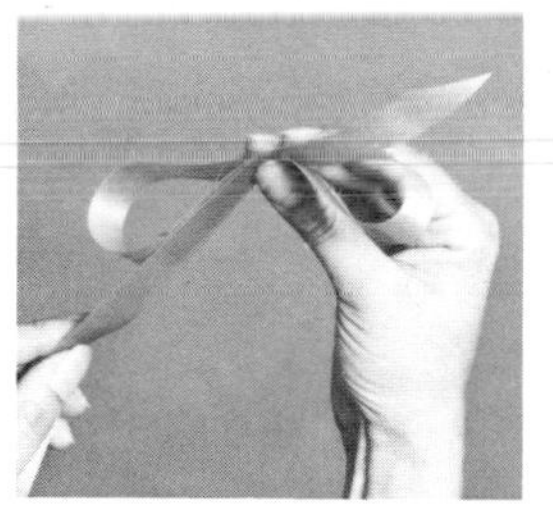

1. Fold the ribbon to the required size so that you have three layers.

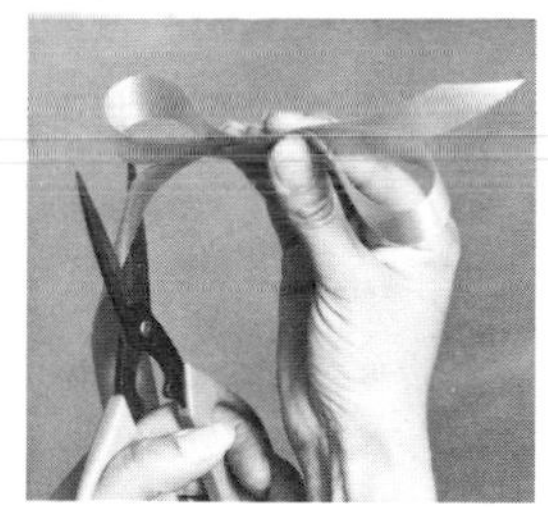

2. Cut off the remaining ribbon.

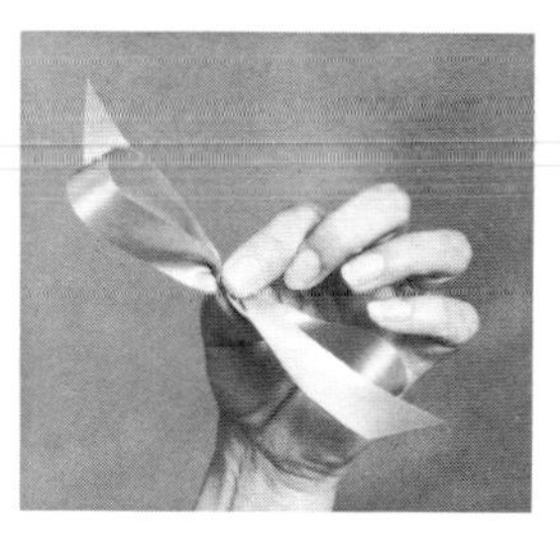

3. Pinch the centre of the ribbon together tightly.

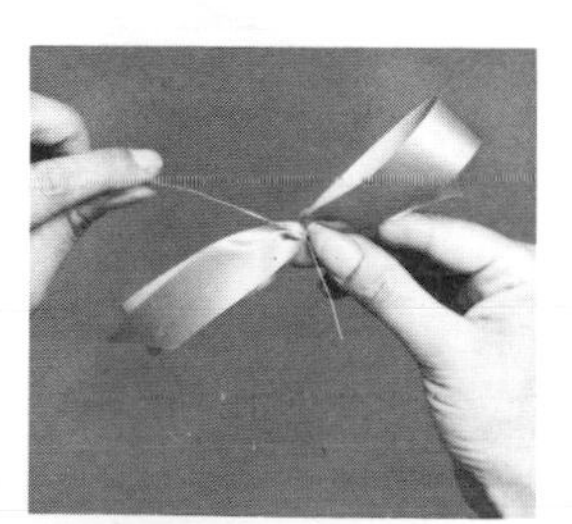

4. Twist a fine silver wire firmly around the pinched ribbon.

5. Twist one wire leg around the other a couple of times.

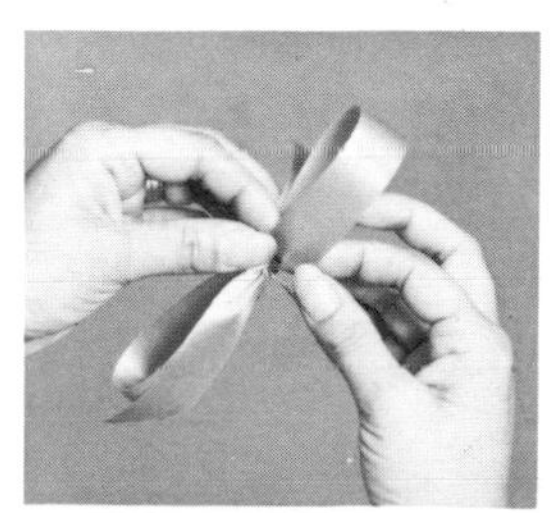

6. Pull the loops into shape.

The shapes to follow

The traditional arrangements will be more pleasing to the eye if it fits into one of the 'basic shapes' which flower arrangers find so useful.

If you can keep your material within one of the outlines shown here you should end up with good proportions, line and balance.

All arrangements should have a height which balances its width and you should choose material which naturally falls easily into the shape you have chosen.

If you are a beginner the 'Symmetrical Triangle' or the 'Circular All-Round' shapes are the easiest to master. After you feel more confident, the curved outlines are well worth attempting.

These suggested shapes are presented to help, but not to restrict your own creativity. If you achieve a shape which is pleasing but doesn't fall within these guidelines so well and good. Remember that your arrangement is there to please you and your family – beauty is in the eye of the beholder.

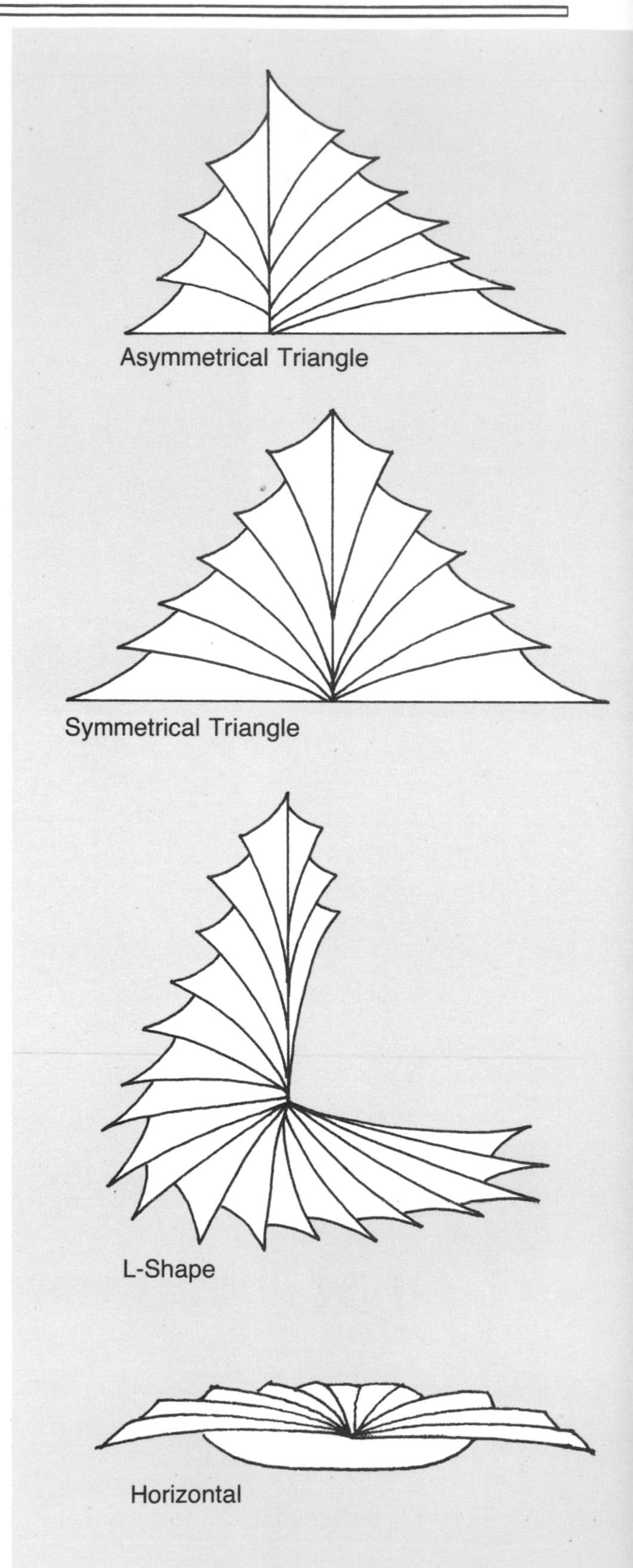

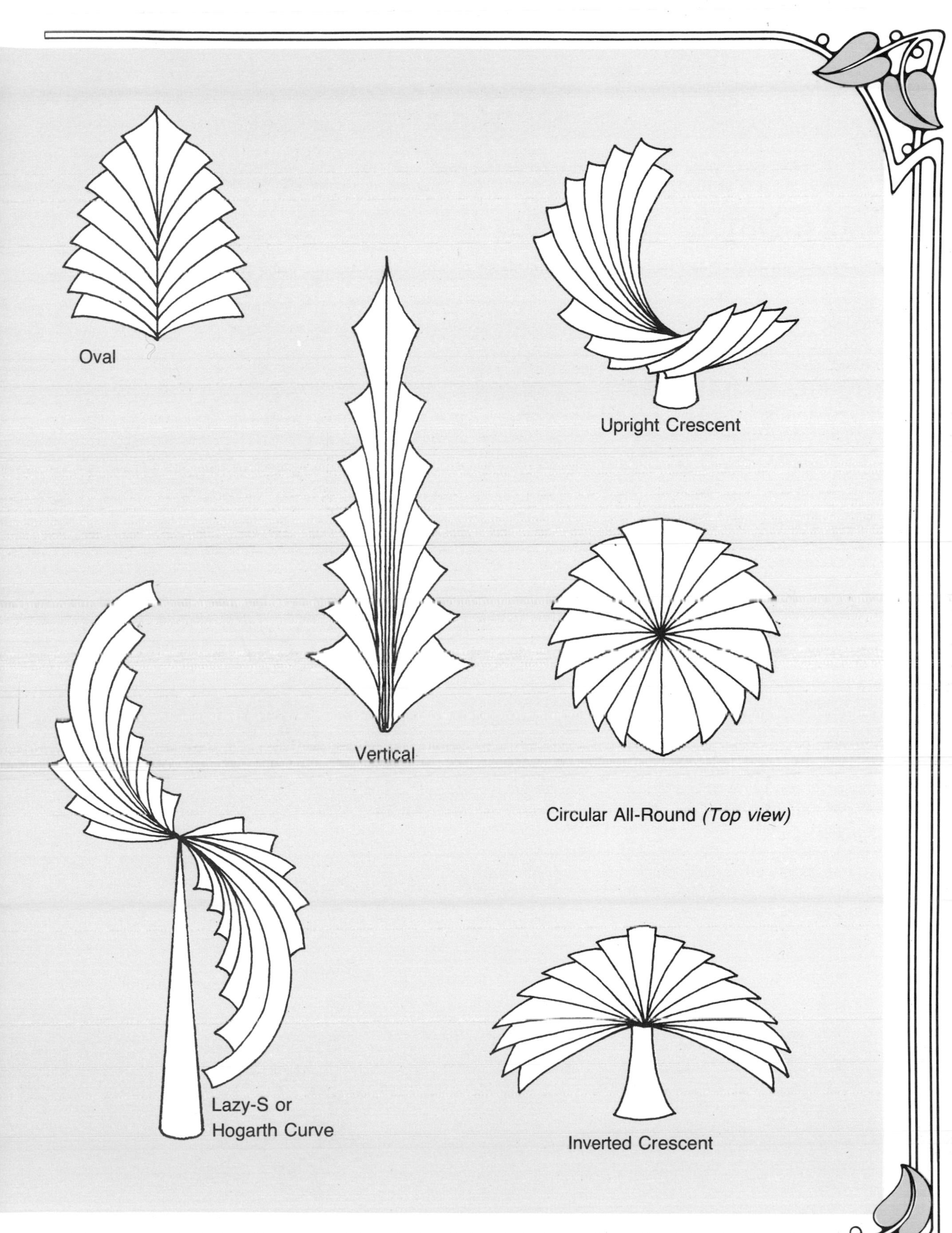
Oval
Vertical
Upright Crescent
Circular All-Round (Top view)
Lazy-S or
Hogarth Curve
Inverted Crescent

Lotus Eaters

The dramatic impact of these lotus blooms is based on simplicity of a vertical line and the beauty of the flowers.

How it is made

Fix the plasticine anchor into the centre of the dish and push in a ball of Dri-Hard so that the dish is nearly full.

The first stem is cut to the required length, which in this decoration was 24 inches. You will need a pair of pliers and perhaps some extra muscle power to cut through these stems – florist cutters are not up to the job. Leave the flower petals as if in the bud stage and position vertically in the Dri-Hard (Fig. 1).

The next lotus stem is cut to length so the slightly open petals are a couple of inches below the base of the tallest flower. Position this flower slightly to the left and pointing slightly towards the front (Fig. 2).

The last flower is cut very short. Each petal of these flowers is individually wired so you will be able to open the petals to give a full-blown effect. The third flower faces the front and is slightly to the right hand side of the vertical.

You should have three leaves left from the stem of the third flower. Wire each of the leaves individually and use to fill in around the base. When dry cover the Dri-Hard with small stones or shingle.

Stand the arrangement on an oval smoked glass dish or a leaf plate and add an oriental figure to complete the picture.

Variations

There are various other large blooms including pink magnolia which you could use in a similar way. Keep the scale of the total arrangement in keeping with the size of the individual blooms.

Fig. 1

Fig. 2

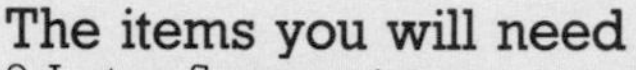

The items you will need

3 Lotus flower stems
1 Black dish (at least 1 inch deep)
Plasticine anchor, Oasis fix
Dri-Hard, stones or shingle
1 Pair of pliers

Apricot & Cream

The delight of this decoration is the various different sizes of roses in a soft shade of apricot which would compliment any room. The shape is attractive and easily copied.

How it is made

The delphiniums provide the basic points of the arrangement. The first stem of apricot colour is cut to length which should be approximately 1½ times the height of the container. This is positioned centrally in the ball of Dri-Hard fixed in the top of the container. The other two points of the triangle are made from apricot delphiniums cut shorter than the main stem and bent into shape. If bending these stems is difficult cut them off completely and add a new wire stem which can be twisted easily. The two cream delphiniums are cut even a little shorter and positioned to right and left of the top point (Fig. 1).

Use individual branches of the cream flowers to make six more points of the triangle edges. The three pieces of ivy foliage are used next to offset the rigid upright triangle and to give a softer shape (Fig. 2).
Add nine roses to complete the side outlines. Use buds and medium sized roses starting at the top (Fig. 3). Take the stem of 6 roses and cut off the bottom three. Use the stem to give a trailing point to the left hand side of the base.

Take the three large roses and place as shown in the centre of the arrangement. Three more rose buds complete the main shape.

Now fill in between the roses with branches of cream flowers making sure some of them extend further than others. This avoids a 'flat' look when everything is positioned in the same plane.

The items you will need

3 Stems of apricot delphinium
2 Stems of cream delphinium
3 Stems of small cream flowers
(9 branches per stem)
3 Large apricot roses
6 Medium apricot roses
6 Stems of apricot rose buds
1 Stem of roses
(6 flowers per stem)
1 Wrought iron stand
1 Plasticine anchor, Dri-Hard.

To finish off, fill in the back with the spare roses and a little foliage so that the mechanics are hidden.

Variations

The use of all white flowers contrasted with variegated ivy would work extremely well in this shape and using a black container.

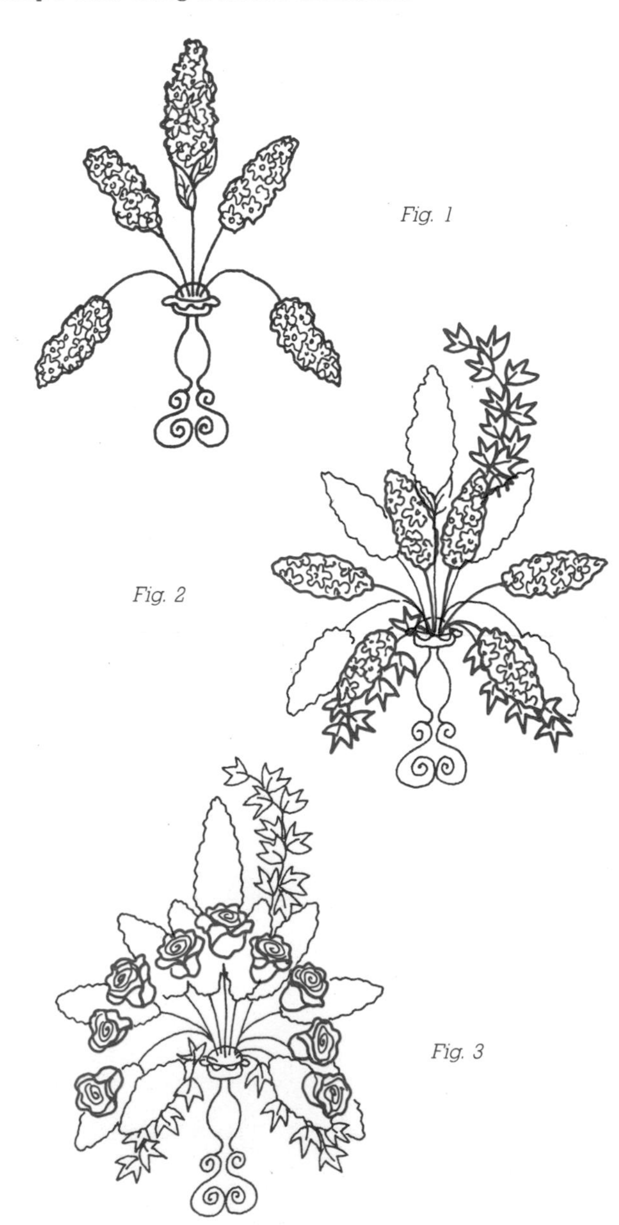

Silk Curves

This may look difficult, but the lazy-S shape of the Hogarth curve is easy to make if you follow the step-by-step instructions carefully.

How it is made

Push a ball of Dri-Hard into the top of the container. The two stems of broom are cut to identical length and curved to give the lazy-S shape. The top piece is positioned slightly at the back of the Dri-Hard while the lower piece is positioned at the front.

Two hyacinth spikes are cut short and used on the back right hand edge and front left hand edge (Fig. 1). These provide a balance and a useful measure so that none of the flowers are positioned outside the narrow shape.

The two rose buds are positioned halfway along each curve. Four daisies provide the central weight and short pieces of broom provide extra points to the curve (Fig. 2).

The four medium roses are positioned next. The largest rose is positioned as the central focal point. Fill in with small pieces of broom between the roses so that the centre is broken up with spiky stems.

At the back keep to the same curved shape and cover the mechanics with any flowers that are left over.

Variations

Pink may not be your choice you you should be able to find alternative flowers in a different shade which all match. Much will depend on the colour of the broom which is available, but yellow and white are possible variations.

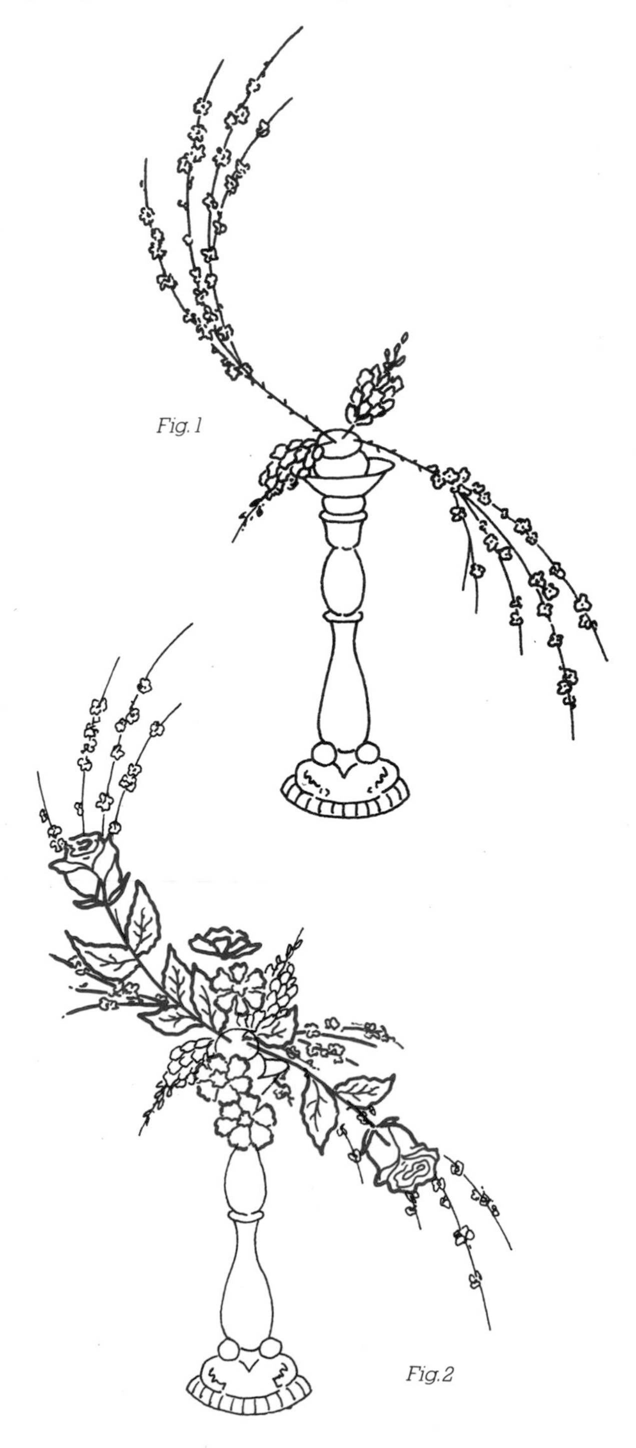

Fig. 1

Fig. 2

The items you will need

2 Sprays of white broom
2 Pink hyacinth sprays
2 Pink rose buds
2 Stems of pink daisies
4 Medium roses
1 Large rose
1 Slender and tall soapstone container
Dri-Hard

Iris & Pussy Willow

This vertical arrangement has the crisp outlines of spring and the cool look of a sophisticated decoration.

How it is made

Fill the neck of the container with Dri-Hard and create the basic shape with four stems of pussy willow. Cut each to length and position at the back of the container as shown in Figure 1.

Next cut and position the five iris as shown in the photograph. Start with the first three as shown in Figure 2. The remaining pussy willow is fixed so that it radiates from a point which is taken as the centre of the lowest iris.

Wire individual leaves of ivy and use to surround the central flower and to emphasise the focal point. Fill in with leaf loops to fill any gaps or cover any bare stems.

To cover the mechanics at the back of the arrangement use any remaining ivy foliage or leaf loops.

Variations

Yellow or white iris will give a more summery look and the pussy willow comes in a warm cream colour instead of ivory grey.

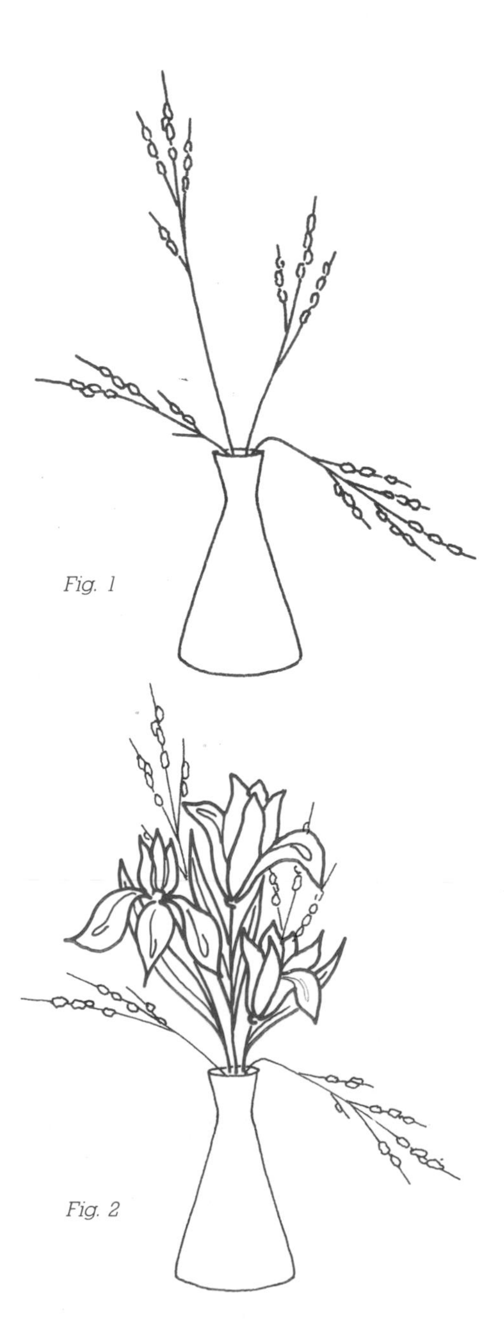

Fig. 1

Fig. 2

The items you will need

1 Stem ivy foliage
5 Blue iris
7 Stems of pussy willow
1 Tall slender container
Dri-Hard

Peach Delight

This delightfully simple arrangement clearly shows how selecting flowers of different sizes in the same colour can provide a natural look. The L-shape is soft and ideally balanced.

How it is made

Stick the anchor in the centre of the wrought iron stand with Oasis fix and push onto the anchor a ball of plasticine.

The first three placements will create the outer points of the L-shape so take care to get these stems positioned correctly (Fig. 1). The first stem in the centre may need support to keep it upright and a double-leg support wire was added in this decoration. The support wire was run from half way up the stem down to the base and then covered with stem wrap.

Cut the second stem shorter and bend slightly so that the outer flower overlaps the edge of the container. The third point of the triangle is one rose cut from a stem of three and wired with a single rose leaf.

Fill in the left hand edge of the arrangement. Two stems, each with three roses, are used at the top and then two individual roses each wired with a leaf are used at the bottom. Similar single roses are wired with a leaf and used to form the base line (Fig. 2). To fill in the triangular shape use several spare leaves each wired and stem-wrapped.

Now place the three large roses starting with the top one. They should all point in different directions to give character to the decoration. The final placement is the stem of three roses positioned on the right hand side to complete a smooth outline.

Use the three roses over and some of the leaves to fill in at the back of the arrangement.

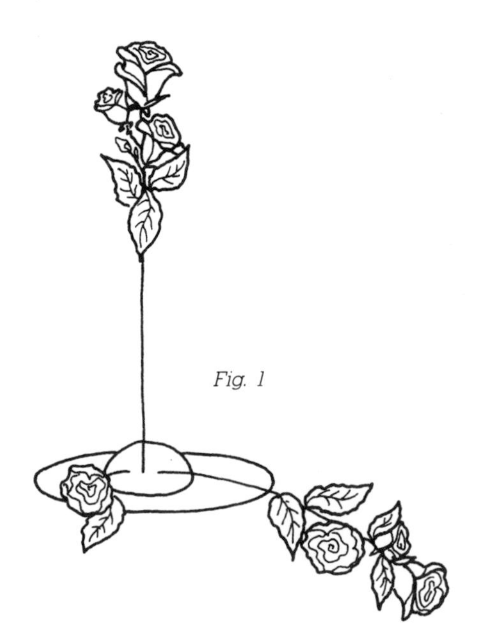

Fig. 1

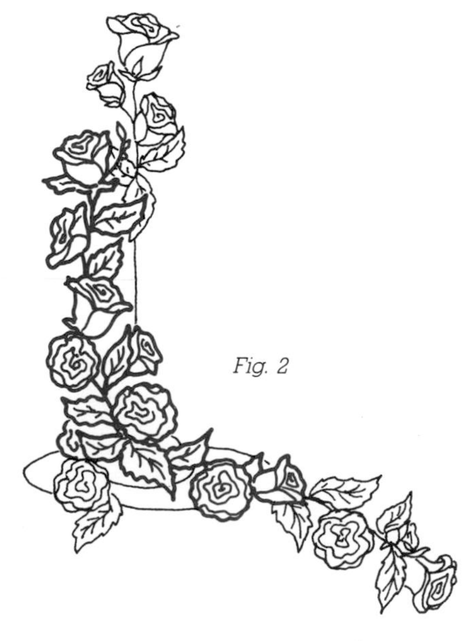

Fig. 2

The items you will need

8 Stems of small roses (3 blooms per stem)
3 Large roses
1 Black wrought iron stand
Plasticine anchor, Oasis fix
Plasticine, Wire, Stemwrap

Variations

Roses are available in many different shades and you can use yellow, cream or white just as effectively. The beauty of this arrangement is in this simple design and the use of flowers of one shade.

Ruby Woodslice

This warm and delightful arrangement uses different flowers of various sizes which all blend together to create the traditional triangular shape.

How it is made

Stick the plasticine anchor in the centre of the woodslice using Oasis fix or similar. Make a ball of plasticine and push this firmly onto the anchor.

The first stem to place is an uncut stem of small azalea which is positioned centrally and vertically. The next two stems of the same flower are cut in half. The top halves, which each have eight flowers, are used to make the base points of the triangle and the bottom halves, which now have two flowers each, are used to create the side outline (Fig. 1).

Now take two stems of the large azalea flowers and cut down the stems in a similar way so that the pieces with five blooms are positioned towards the top edge of the triangle and the pieces with four blooms are used along the base line (Fig. 2).

Place the large roses next. Cut and position the top rose first, then the two side ones, finishing off with the bottom and centre roses. Fill in with carnations cut to length. Any flowers or foliage left over should be used to hide the mechanics at the back.

Fig. 1

Variations

By substituting pale pink roses a completely softer look will be created. Make sure that the colours contrast sufficiently or it may look as if the matching of flowers has been carried out inexpertly.

Fig. 2

The items you will need

4 Stems of small azalea flowers
(10 blooms per stem)
3 Stems of large azalea flowers
(9 blooms per stem)
3 Stems of carnations (4 blooms per stem)
5 Large roses
1 Large woodslice
Plasticine anchor, Oasis fix, Plasticine

Prelude in A Major

Tropical Dish

Some people are unlucky with pot plants – but this delightful trough of artificial ones will sit happily on a windowsill needing no attention at all. These plants will thrive in the most difficult of positions when live plants would certainly die.

How it is made

Fix the two anchors to the base of the trough and push a ball of plasticine onto each. The ivy stems are the first placements. A complete stem goes at the back left, the other stem is cut into two pieces and positioned on the right, the longest piece pointing forwards (Fig. 1).

The Saintpaulia plant is positioned next on the right hand side (Fig. 2). You may find that the long thick stem prevents the plant being positioned close to the rim when you are using a shallow dish. If so, do as we did – cut the stem with wire cutters down to the length required and bunching the pieces together again, re-wire around the stems.

Now position the spiky-leaved Bromeliad at the back left and then position the front two plants. Arrange the leaves of the Fittonia and Tradescantia so that some of them 'grow' over the rim of the dish. Turn the arrangement around and bend the leaves at the back so that any mechanics are hidden and an attractive outline is created.

Helpful Hint

To hide the mechanics use small shingle, Chipped 'Forest Bark' or dry peat to fill the dish. This will provide a natural surface to complete the illusion of growing plants.

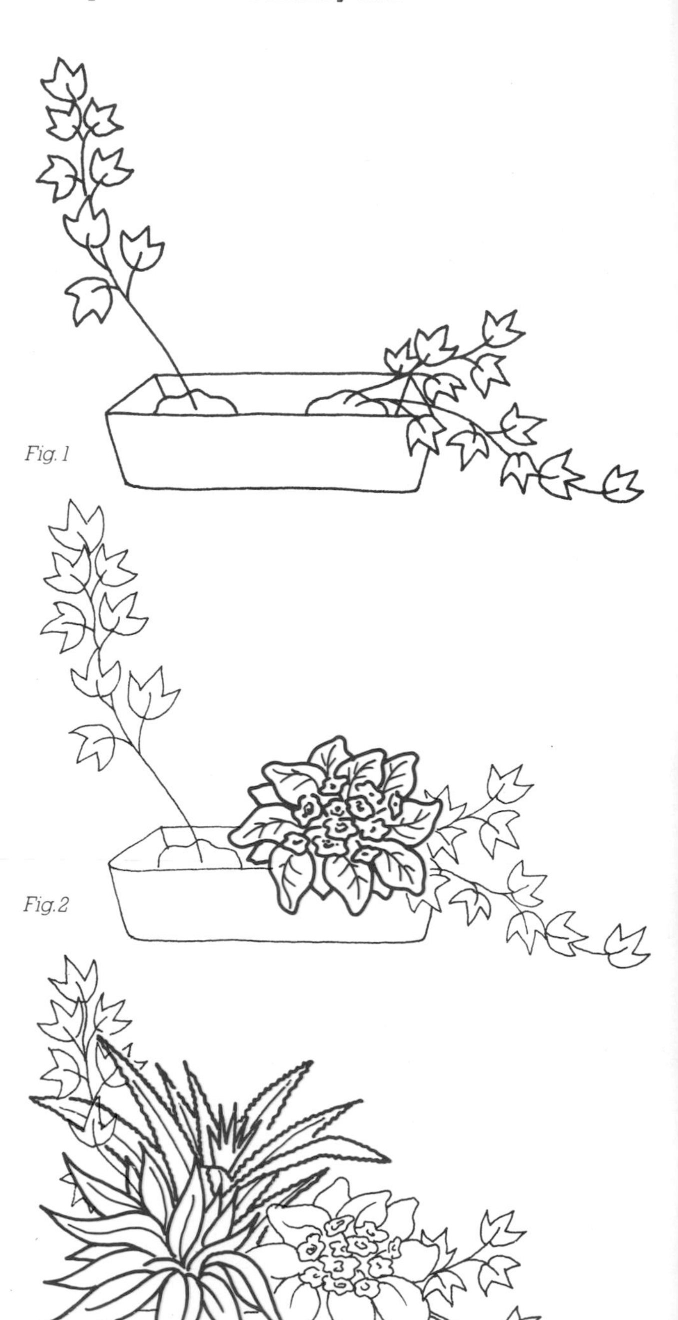

The items you will need

2 Stems of variegated ivy
1 Saintpaulia (African Violet)
1 Fittonia (Snakeskin plant)
1 Bromeliad/Gazmania
1 Tradescantia (Wandering Jew)
1 Small trough
2 Plasticine anchors, Oasis fix, Plasticine

Pink Crescent

The inverted crescent shape is well complimented by the attractive black vase. This is a standard shape which can be used in many situations.

How it is made

Fix the plasticine anchor in the vase with Oasis fix and fill with Dri-Hard. Start the arrangement with the top most daisy stem cut to approximately six inches tall and positioned centrally. The two outer trailing points of the crescent are made by daisies. Bend the stems at right angles so that the flowers are positioned well below the rim of the vase (Fig. 1).

Use two daisy stems and two zinnias to complete the top edge of the arrangement. The base of the shape is made with two stems of daisies, each stem bent at right angles to get the flowers pointing in the right direction (Fig. 2).

The low central zinnia flowers are positioned next. Make sure that each faces a slightly different way (Fig. 3).

Fill in the shape with the remaining daisy flowers, recessing some of the flowers so that their heads are close to the Dri-Hard.

Fig. 2

Fig. 3

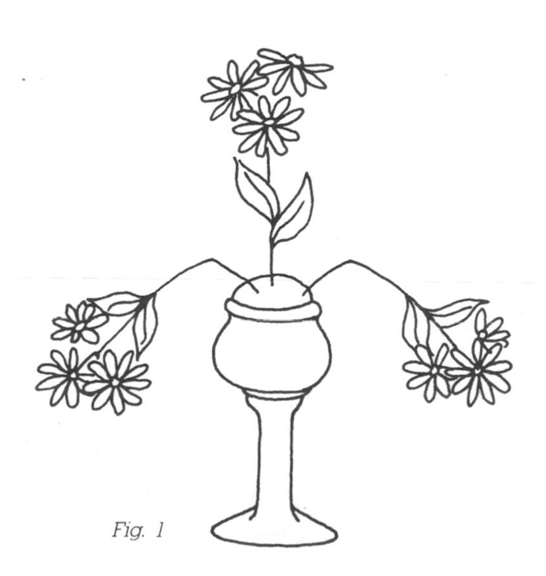

Fig. 1

Variations

Shades of lilac and white look stunning in a black dish and would match the simple elegance of the container.

The items you will need

4 Stems of pink daisies (3 branches per stem)
2 Stems of large pink zinnias
(3 flowers per stem)
1 Black vase
Plasticine anchor, Oasis fix, Dri-Hard

Summer Sun

This is a most useful design where a low all-round shape is needed. The various shades of light hearted lemon and white will blend in almost all positions.

How it is made

The circular shape is important and the equal length of the six stems of lily-of-the-valley is important. Cut the first stem, check it is the right length by pushing into the ball of Dri-Hard fixed to the middle of the saucer with a plasticine anchor. When the length of the first stem is correct, remove and cut the other five stems exactly to match. Position close to the saucer as shown (Fig. 1).

The height of the arrangement is governed by the first centrally positioned gerbera. It should be approximately the same length as the lily-of-the-valley stems. Around, but below this central flower position two lemon carnations and two gerberas (Fig. 2).

Between each lily-of-the-valley flower, position a lemon carnation shorter than those six stems (Fig. 3).

Place the white chrysanthemums cut and wired individually between the top and bottom circle of flowers and then fill in any gaps with pieces of small yellow flowers.

Spare flowers are cut very short and recessed close to the Dri-Hard. In this way the mechanics are covered but the overall airy look of the arrangements is maintained.

Terms Explained

Recessing

In some arrangements there is a tendancy to create a flat outer face of flowers. To add depth and dimension cut some stems much shorter than others and push into the base of the arrangement. This is known as recessing.

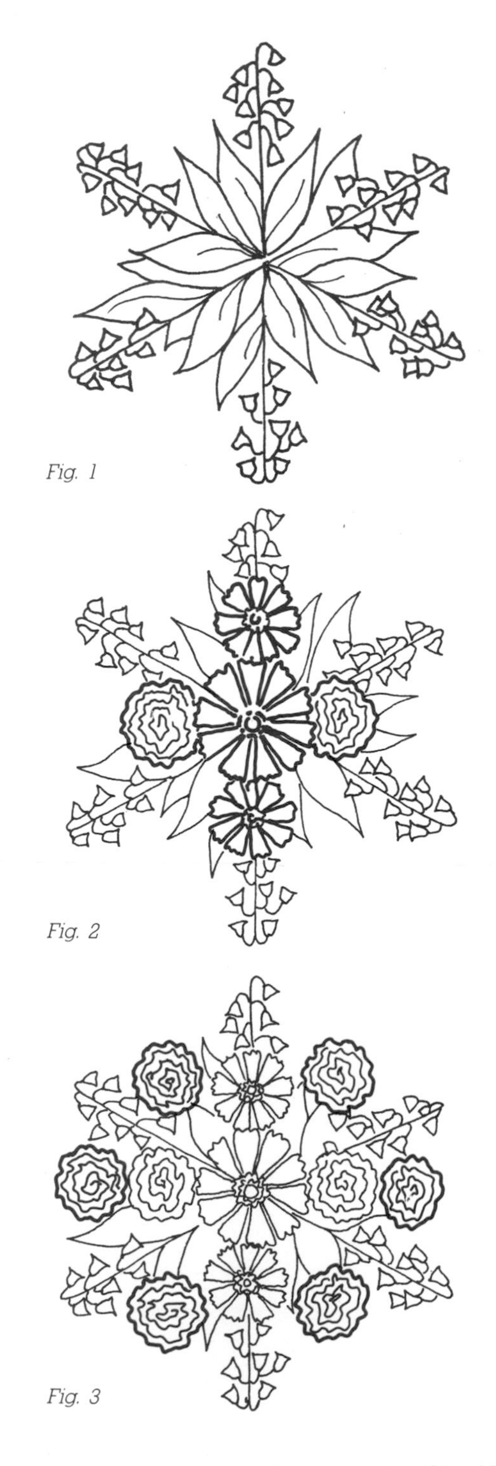

Fig. 1

Fig. 2

Fig. 3

The items you will need

3 White gerberas
6 Stems of lily-of-the-valley
8 Lemon carnations
2 Stems of small yellow flowers
2 Stems of white chrysanthemums
(6 flowers per stem)
1 White saucer
Plasticine anchor, Oasis fix, Dri-Hard

Pink Sensation

Selecting the various shades of pink for each flower type is important. The illusion of reality is created by choosing three different shades of carnations and lilies and two shades of gladioli.

How it is made

Use Oasis fix to stick the plasticine anchor in the centre of the dish. Push a ball of Dri-Hard onto the anchor.

Cut the two longest gladioli stems to leave three flowers and a bud with sufficient stem to go into the Dri-Hard. Position these at the ends of the rectangle. The side flowers of gladioli are much shorter, with one flower and buds left per stem.

Use single branches of lily flowers to the sides of each of the longer points as shown in Figure 1.

Position the first carnation centrally on a short stem. The height of this carnation will determine the overall shape of this arrangement so spend time getting it right.

Use four carnations cut short to create the oval plan of the decoration (Fig. 2). Now cover the stems of these four carnations with a branch of lily flowers cut a little shorter.

The four carnations which surround the central flower are positioned next, followed by the two carnations which are positioned over the longest gladioli.

Now fill in with lily flowers and recess with single gladioli blooms close to the Dri-Hard. Wire remaining gladioli foliage and position as necessary.

Fig. 1

Fig. 2

The items you will need

4 Pink gladioli
6 Stems of pink lilies
(2 branches per stem)
11 Pink carnations
1 Low rectangular plastic dish
Plasticine anchor, Oasis fix, Dri-Hard

Variations

These flowers are available in other colour combinations. Various shades of orange and yellow are popular in these flower types. Remember that for a dinner party the central flower could be replaced by a matching candle.

Spring Profusion

The bright freshness of this arrangement would make a delightful gift for someone in hospital. The pinks and blues would be appropriate in the maternity ward.

How it is made

The centre stem of light blue iris is approximately 18 inches tall. The side points of the triangle are made from white freesias, each cut to approximately 9 inches long (Fig. 1).

Next take two more light blue iris, four pink carnations and one freesia and position as shown in Figure 2.

Position the three dark blue iris next and then more stems of white freesias, all radiating from the central point. Fill in with carnations, varying the shades next to each other as you progress.

Fill in around the base of the stems with single freesia flowers each wired separately on a short stem. At the back of the arrangement fill in with leaf loops (Fig. 3), made from iris foliage plus a few freesia flowers to hide the mechanics.

Fig.2

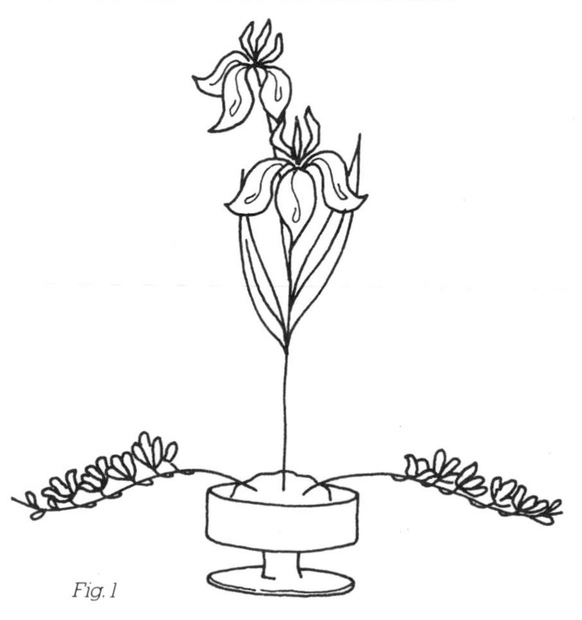

Fig.1

Fig. 3

The items you will need

3 Light blue iris (2 flowers per stem)
3 Dark blue iris (single flowers)
5 Stems pink carnations (4 flowers per stem)
7 Sprays of white freesias
1 White pedestal dish
Plasticine anchor, Dri-Hard

Variations

Any combinations of spring flowers would look nice, but the inclusion of yellow iris will add a bright sunny look which you may appreciate.

Poppy Fields

Even kitchen dishes can prove most useful as containers for arrangements. These delightful poppies are displayed in a small casserole dish with lid, set on a cane place mat.

How it is made

Fix the anchor in the bottom of the dish and then push onto it a ball of plasticine or Dri-Hard. Next position the lid against the container with a piece of plasticine so that you know the shape of the base you are using.

Use ivy stems to create the three outer points of the triangle. The central line is made with one stem (2 branches). The lower two with pieces cut to length and bent over the rim (Fig. 1).

The first poppy to place is the top one which is slightly right of centre. Work from the top and aim to use four poppies to amplify the triangular shape (Fig. 2).

Now complete the centre with poppies, making sure each points in a slightly different direction. Now position the poppy buds and the rest of the ivy to fill in and complete the shape.

Keep one or two buds and a few pieces of ivy foliage to tidy up the back of the arrangement.

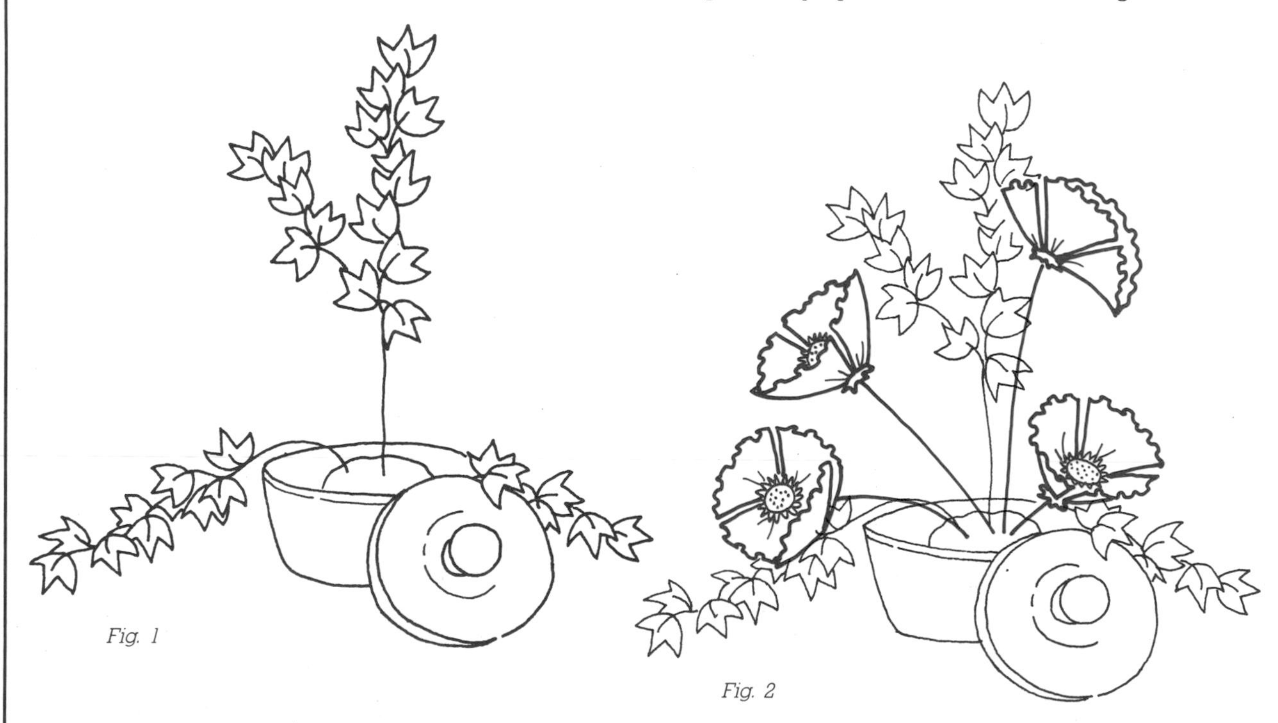

Fig. 1

Fig. 2

The items you will need

7 Red poppies
4 Stems of ivy (2 branches per stem)
1 Red dish with lid
Plasticine anchor, Oasis fix, Plasticine

Variations

Poppies are available in both orange and white colours. You will obviously need to change the colour of the dish to blend in with the tone of your choice.

You could also add a few stems of honey-coloured wheat or barley to hint at the normal location of these delightful flowers.

Days of Spring

Just a few flowers and a twist of a branch can create a wistful look of the promise of spring.

How it is made

Place the anchor slightly left of centre and push on a ball of plasticine. The first thing to position is the twig. The circular shape at the base is not natural and we have wired one of the branches to the bottom of the stem so that it stays in this attractive position.

Follow the picture opposite and position the first four flowers in this order. The tallest iris is positioned at the back, slightly to the left of centre (Fig. 1), next the tallest daffodil followed by the centre and lowest daffodil. The positioning of these flowers will create a slightly curved line which runs happily from top right to bottom left (Fig. 2).

The stem of the lowest iris is cut short and positioned directly below the centre daffodil (Fig. 3).

Take one stem of snowdrops, cut short and position to the left of the arrangement. The other stem is split into two bunches, each wired separately. One bunch goes at the back on the right hand side – the other centre front.

Cover the mechanics with moss and if you have a china lamb, use this to complete the picture.

Variations

Use an Oasis round for fresh flowers and use fresh stems of pussy willow to add interesting catkins to this delightful spring arrangement.

Fig. 1

Fig. 2

Fig. 3

What you will need

2 Stems of blue iris
3 Daffodils
2 Stems of snowdrops
1 Twig of corkscrew willow
1 China Dish
Plasticine anchor, Oasis fix, Plasticine, Moss

Bowl of Plants

There are many artificial pot plants available nowadays and when grouped attractively they make a permanent display which never needs watering. Here is a grouping which makes a delightful gift.

How it is made

Fix three plasticine anchors in the bottom of the bowl and use large balls of Dri-Hard to cover most of the floor of the bowl (Fig. 1).

Follow the plans shown here to achieve a pleasant contrast of colours and leaf textures.

The Sanseviera (1) is first positioned towards the back, then the Cyclamen (2) and then the red Dracaena (3).

The African Violet (4) and Euonymus (5) are positioned to the front so that the leaves overlap the rim of the bowl (Fig. 3). The trailing ivy plant is split into two pieces which are used in positions 6 and 7. Finally the small-leaved ivy plant is used at the back in position 8.

When the Dri-Hard has set you can start to move individual leaves so that they make natural curves and twists. Now you can fill the bowl with shingle to create a natural 'soil' level and hide the Dri-Hard.

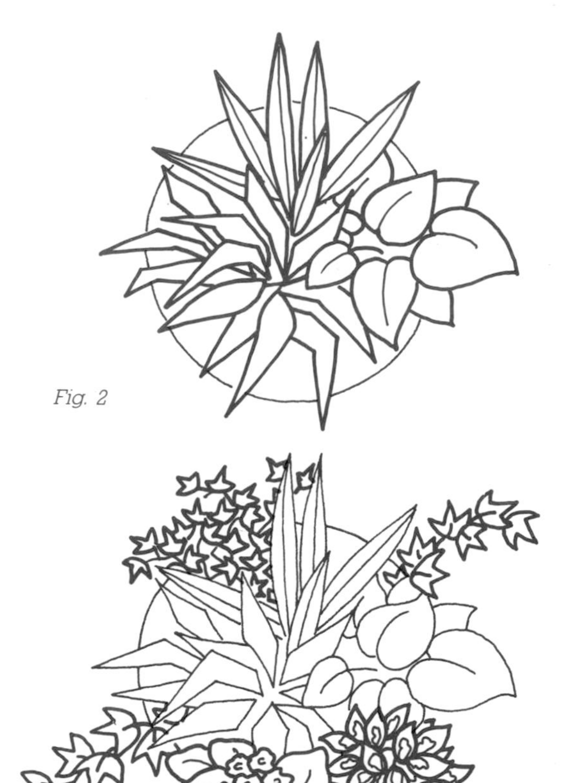

Fig. 2

Fig. 3

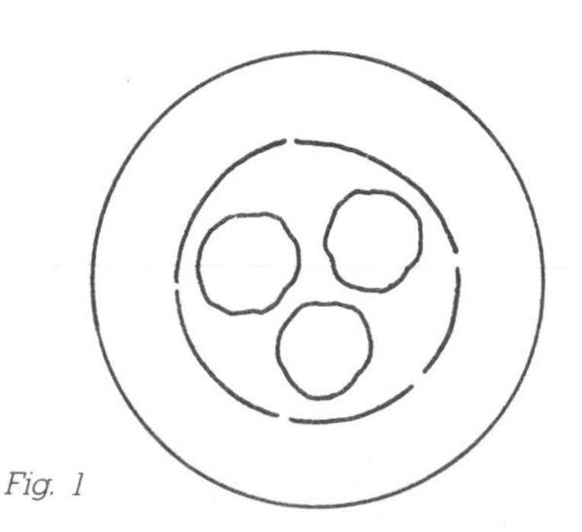

Fig. 1

The items you will need

1 Sanseviera (Mother-in-law's Tongue)
1 Cyclamen
1 Dracaena (Flaming Dragon Tree)
1 Saintpaulia (African violet)
1 Variegated Euonymus
1 Trailing Ivy plant
1 Small leaved Ivy plant
1 Large bowl
3 Plasticine anchors, Oasis fix,
Dri-Hard, Shingle

Variations

Choose any houseplants which have contrasting foliage colour and shapes and which have different heights. Always bear in mind the size of the bowl and use enough houseplants to fill the container.

Chelsea Boot

Containers don't have to be conventional to be acceptable. Here is a china button boot which has been topped off with warm russet foliage and flowers which sits prettily in this Victorian 'What-Not'.

How it is made

Fill the top of the boot with plasticine leaving a smooth rounded surface.

The basic shape is an offset triangle and this is created with three pieces of fern foliage. The first piece is the top of a stem which has three leaves. This is placed to the back pointing slightly backwards and toward the left.

The other two pieces are individual leaves which have had wire 'legs' added (Fig. 1). Complete the outline with two smaller pieces of fern (Fig. 2).

Now start to position the roses all pointing in a different direction. Start with the top bud and then the right hand bud. Work from the top with the larger flowers and fill in the triangle shape with the occasional rose leaf as appropriate (Fig. 3).

Fill in between the roses with apricot blossom using small bunches of a few flowers for each bunch. You may find that small pieces of fern are also needed between the roses.

Now turn the arrangement around and use some of the blossom and some foliage to hide the mechanics.

Terms Explained

A 'leg' is simply an added stem created by twisting wire as shown on page 15.

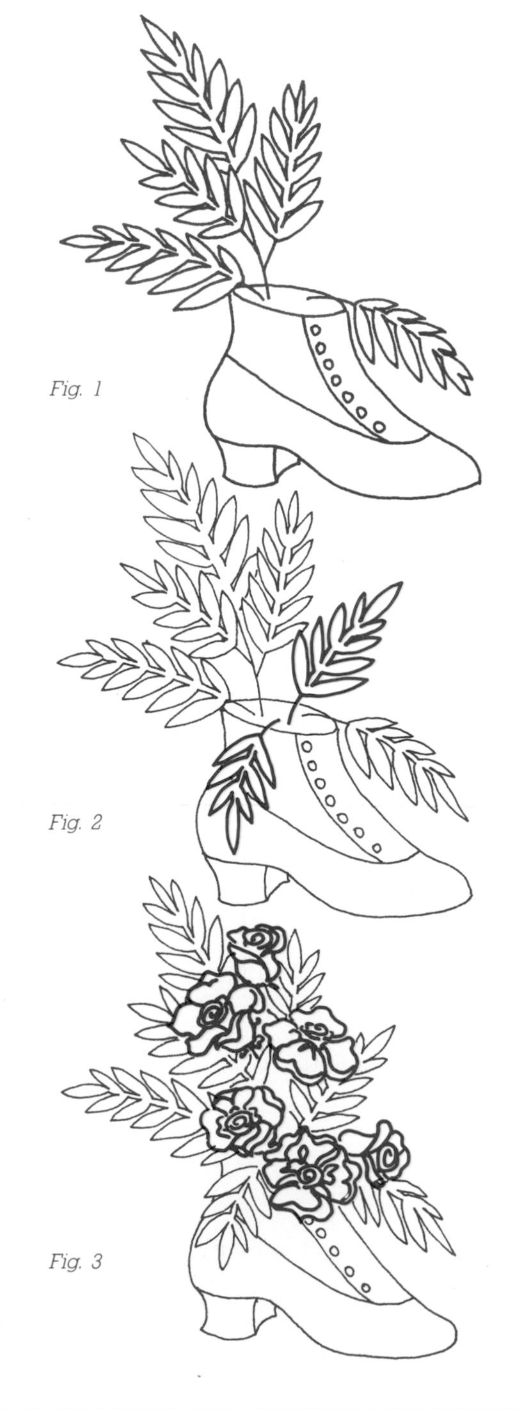

Fig. 1

Fig. 2

Fig. 3

The items you will need

2 Stems of rose (3 flowers per stem)
1 Stem of apricot blossom
(3 branches per stem)
2 Stems of autumn fern (7 leaves per stem)
1 China boot
Plasticine

Handful of Freesias

This deceptively simple arrangement of multi-coloured freesias has been kept light and airy by omitting any overpowering foliage.

How it is made

Fix the plasticine anchor to the bottom of the hand vase using Oasis fix. Now add a large ball of plasticine so that the vase is half full of the material.

Start by taking seven stems to create the outer edge of the circular shape. In Figure 1. we have shown how to position these first stems. Note that each stem has a different curve and none are exactly the same length. In this way you start with an informal look which exactly matches the freesia flowers.

Maintain the overall shape and add further stems working towards the centre. Keep the colours separate and radiate the stems from a single point.

We have recommended that you use plasticine as the base of this arrangement because when you have completed the arrangement you may want to change a few stems here and there. Freesias are not easy to arrange, but using a vase with a purpose in life adds much to the overall effect.

Variations

Multi-coloured sweet peas are available in similar shades and could be used to great effect. Make sure each stem is slightly curved to compliment the shape of the hand.

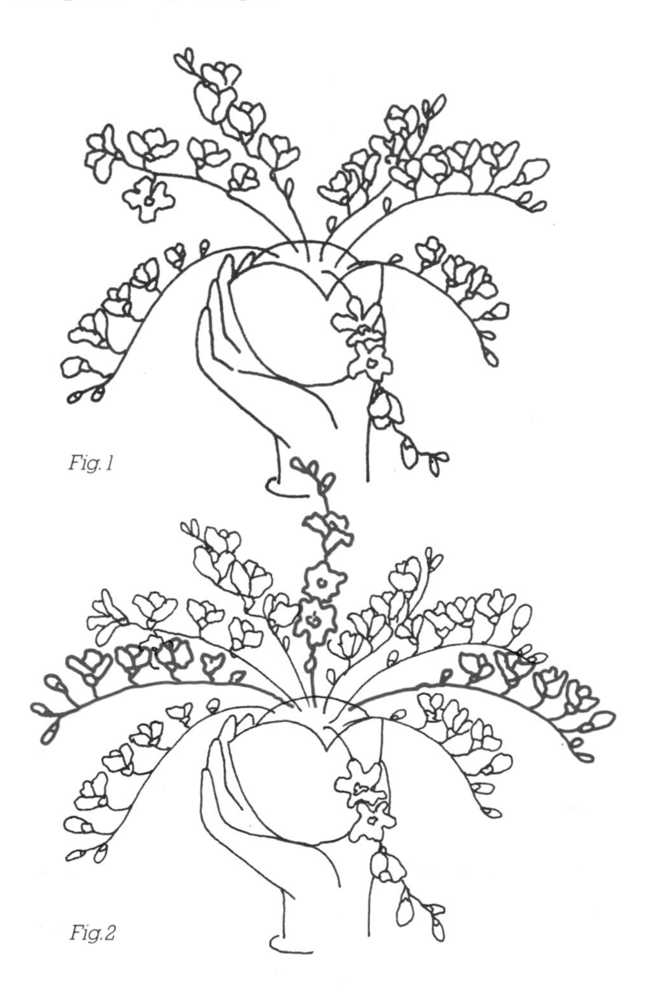

Fig. 1

Fig. 2

The items you will need

21 Freesia stems
1 Hand vase
Plasticine anchor, Oasis fix, Plasticine

Basket of Blue

Filling a basket with flowers is one of the traditional arrangement styles which is very pleasing when you use various flowers of the same basic colour.

How it is made

When arranging the flowers, bear in mind the principle that it should be possible to pick up by the handle any arrangement finished in a basket.

Start by fixing a plasticine anchor to the base of the basket and pushing on a ball of plasticine.

The first three placements are the three stems of blue delphinium which will determine the furthest outline of the arrangement (Fig. 1). The centre piece is cut to be just taller than the handle and is positioned to its right. The other delphiniums overlap the edges of the basket well.

Now position lily-of-the-valley as shown in Figure 2, bending and curving the stems as necessary to give a natural look. With the basic points in position cut the large pale blue carnations to size and arrange them in the centre of the basket. The tallest are at the back, the shortest at the front.

Use small pieces of blue button carnations to complete the outline of the arrangement and the white button carnations in the centre. Lastly position the very dark blue cornflowers to give a contrast at the outer edges of the arrangement, in this way you will find the tones change from white in the centre to dark blue at the edges.

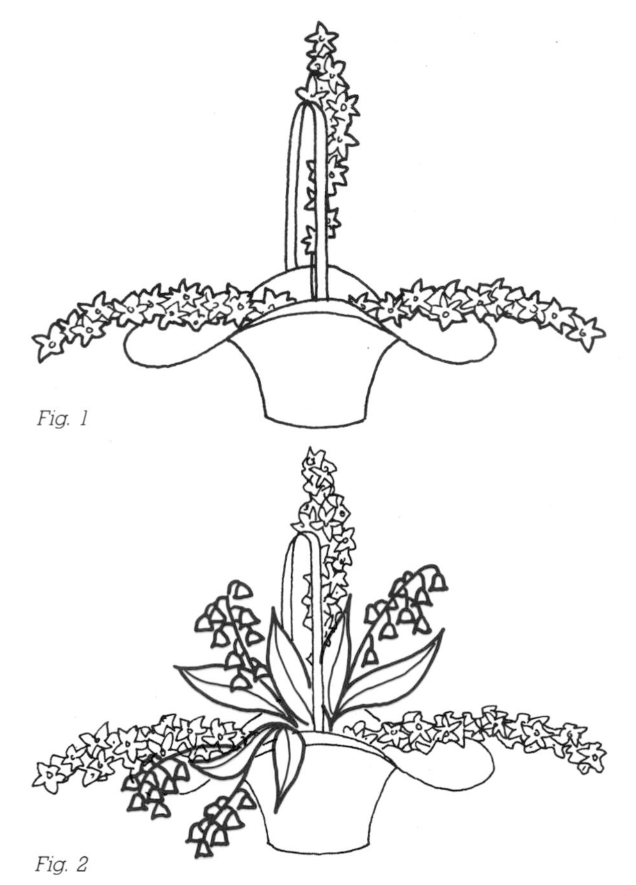

Fig. 1

Fig. 2

Helpful Hint

If you are presenting this basket as a gift, tie a lemon or white bow to the handle.

The items you will need

4 Stems of lily-of-the-valley
4 Stems of delphinium
3 Stems of blue button carnations
2 Stems of white button carnations
1 Stem of cornflower
5 Large pale blue carnations
1 Wicker basket
Plasticine anchor, Plasticine

Trails of Fuchsia

The frivolous look created by the impressive ceramic clown on a swing with tumbling fuchsias is ideal for a safe hanging position where it will become a real eye-catcher.

How it is made

Fix a plasticine anchor inside the well of the container and push on a round of foam for dried flowers. This will avoid the extra weight which plasticine or Dri-Hard would add.

The first three placements (Fig. 1) provide the main points of the arrangement. Start by emphasising the curve of the arm over the clown's head with one branch of a fuchsia plant. It should not hide the arm completely nor cover the face. Now position the first two trailing points using different shades of plants. The stems should hang naturally to display the 'ballerina skirts' of the attractive flowers.

Now position the remaining three stems as shown in Figure 2. The length of the front two pieces is important – they should fall naturally within the points already created in the first stage.

You should next take some of the fuchsia foliage and wire individual leaves. Use them to fill in around the foam so that the stems and mechanics cannot be seen.

Safety Note

With any hanging decoration it is worth investing in proper baskets and fixings which are strong enough for the purpose. Test the fixings before you hang up expensive containers to avoid disaster.

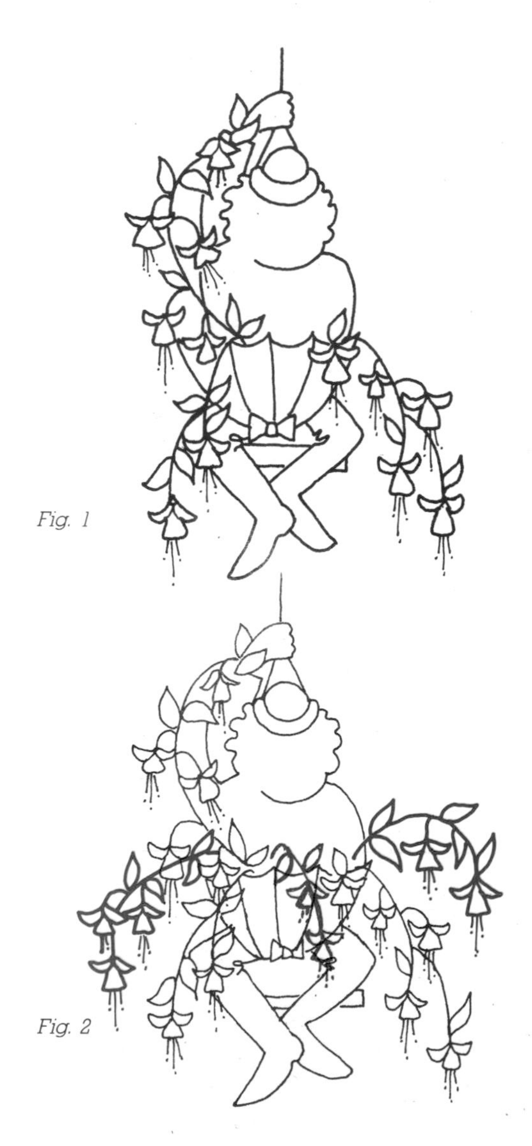

Fig. 1

Fig. 2

The items you will need

3 Fuchsia plants (different colours)
1 Ceramic clown on a swing
Plasticine anchor, Oasis fix,
Oasis foam for dried flowers

Daisy Basket

The yellow roses and creamy daisies informally peeping from this wicker basket could be used anywhere in the home to add a country garden look to the decor.

How it is made

Using the plasticine anchor firmly fixed to the bottom of the basket push in a round of foam to hold dried flowers. You may need to cut this down to size so that the level of your foam is below the rim of the basket.

If the lid is not already fixed in position use pieces of plasticine to wedge it open in an attractive position which is not quite vertical.

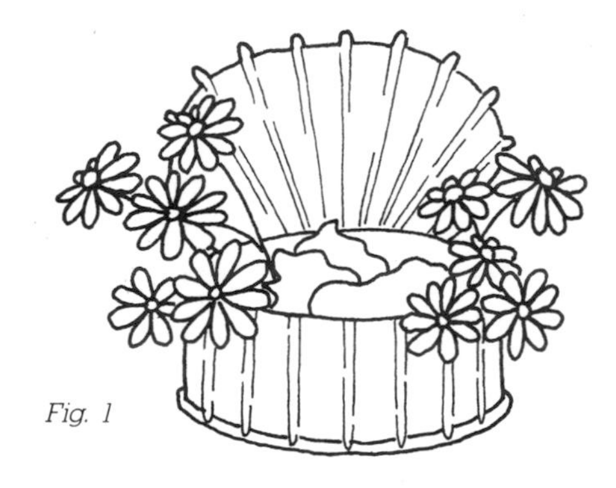

Fig. 1

The first four placements are half stems of daisies placed in the four corners of the basket (Fig. 1). Remember that the front daisies should overlap the edge of the basket.

The next step is to cut the rose stems down in half, add a wire leg to each if necessary and position as shown in Figure 2.

Fig. 2

With the outline created use individual flowers to fill in and complete the shape. Make sure some of the flowers are recessed below the level of the main blooms so that you avoid a flat, one dimensional look.

Variations

Using two flowers of differing form whose colours are chosen with care will work in the tight confines of a basket. Remember that the look is an informal one and you should avoid spikey stems which will ruin the soft lushness of the shape.

The items you will need

3 Stems of cream marguerite daisies (7 flowers per stem)
3 Stems of yellow roses (7 flowers per stem)
Plasticine anchor, Oasis fix,
Oasis foam for dried flowers

Riverside Tulips

This classic shape is well served by the brilliant colour of the chosen tulips and emphasised by the upright bulrushes.

How it is made

Place an anchor in the centre of the base using Oasis fix and then push a ball of plasticine firmly onto it.

Start with the central bulrush which is vertical and then the bulrush to the right. The first tulip is cut next and points slightly left of upright just below the central bulrush (Fig. 1).

Now create the offset triangular shape with two more tulips cut to length (Fig. 2). It is now a simple job to fill in with the rest of the flowers and the third bulrush.

The petals of the final central tulip should be eased open before it is positioned. You may need to use fine silver wire on the back of the petals to ensure the petals stay open.

To complete the shape and the outline use tulip foliage either flat or in 'leaf' loops.

Terms Explained

To make 'leaf' loops simply wire the point of the foliage to the stem to make an attractive shape (Fig. 3). Before placing the leaf bow cover any wire with stemwrap. The technique is simplicity itself and is extremely useful in many arrangements.

Fig. 1

Fig. 2

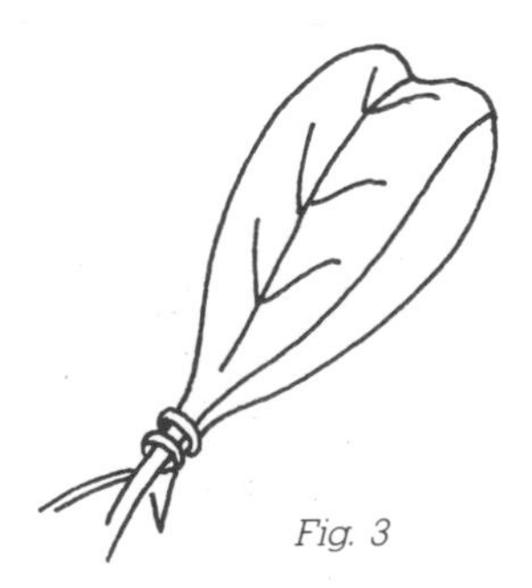

Fig. 3

The items you will need

6 Red tulips
3 Bulrushes (Cat-tails)
Wrought iron base
Plasticine anchor, Oasis fix, Plasticine

Gardenia Cage

High in the air this cage of attractive white gardenia is ideal for a window position, where it catches the afternoon sun.

How it is made

Fix a plasticine anchor in the centre of the base with Oasis fix. Push a ball of plasticine on the anchor. The first three points give the curving shape which overflows the edges of the bird cage. The top point is made by a bud and flower positioned to the left of the container and curved to shape. The two trailing points each with a flower and bud are of different lengths and trail below the base of the cage (Fig. 1).

The positioning of the next gardenia flowers is shown in Figure 2. They accentuate the curved shape and fill the outline.

Now cut the ivy stems into small pieces or individual leaves and wire each part. Use to fill in and amplify the shape. The fittonia stems were taken apart into individual stems and used to fill in the base of the arrangement. Push some of these stems close to the plasticine to hid the mechanics.

Variations

A bird may be used to add colour to the decoration but be careful that it is positioned at a focal point and not somewhere where the balance of the display is disturbed.

Fig. 1

Fig. 2

The items you will need

1 Wrought iron bird cage container
3 Stems of gardenia flowers
1 Fittonia plant
2 Stems of variegated ivy foliage
Plasticine anchor, Plasticine

Golden Lightness

As a change from red and silver this arrangement makes a pleasant alternative for Christmas which can be used for months after.

How it is made

Wrap a piece of plasticine in aluminium foil and position in the holder using an anchor firmly secured with Oasis fix.

Position the candle centrally and vertically in the plasticine after preparing it with cocktail sticks as shown on page 17.

Use the six roses to fix the outside limits and the overall rounded shape of the arrangement (Fig. 1). Use the brown daisies and azalea blooms to fill in the shape, making sure some of the blooms overhang the container. To obtain this overhang effect bend the stem of the flower or foliage. The yellow daisies are used in the centre in a crescent shape (Fig. 2).

Now fill in with the leaves which you will have removed from the other stems. Wire separately and push in close to the plasticine.

Finish off with two double loop bows on the face, either side of centre. The tying of ribbons is shown in detail on page 19.

Variations

Red and pink flowers would create a warm glow to match a candle of the same colour. If you are thinking of Christmas time decoration, silver foliage would also add a touch of sparkle.

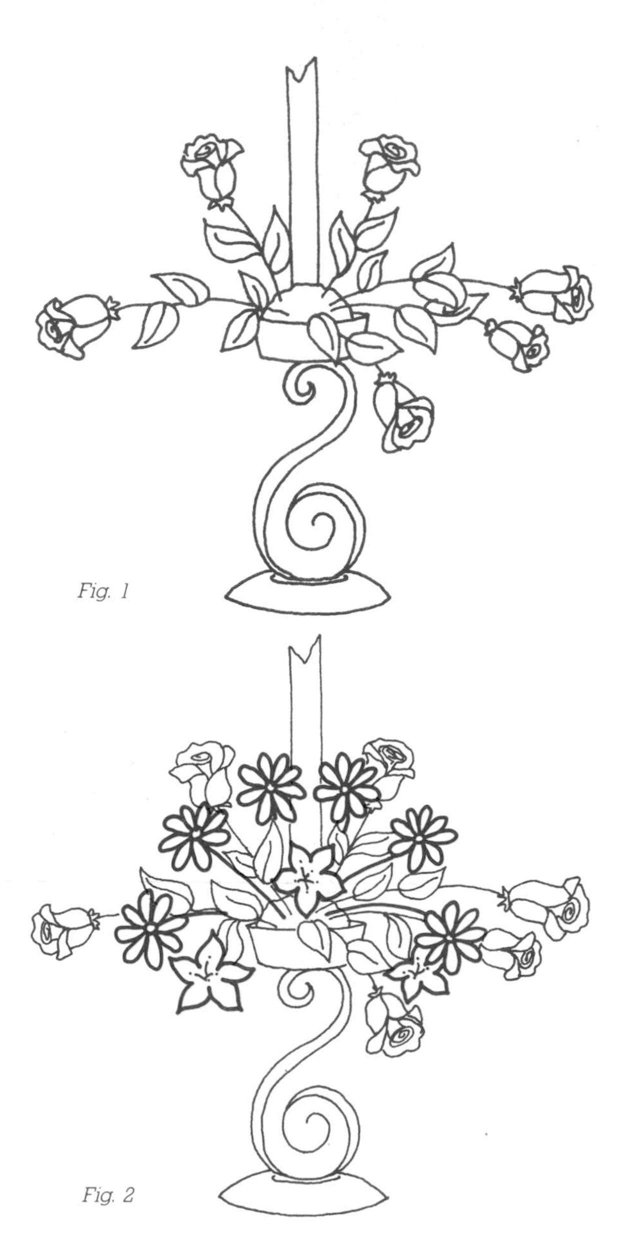

Fig. 1

Fig. 2

The items you will need

3 Gold rose buds
3 Lemon rose buds
6 Yellow daisies
2 Stems brown daisies
3 Stems of azalea blooms
Yellow ribbon
1 Candle
1 Wrought iron base
Plasticine anchor, Oasis fix, Plasticine

Happy Christmas

Alabaster Smoothness

This arrangement proves that overall form can be achieved when similar flowers are grouped in bunches rather than distributed evenly around the arrangement. Different flower shapes which vary in size provide interest and contrast.

How it is made

Fix the plasticine anchor in the centre of the glass dish and push on a ball of plasticine.

Start with three freesias and position them as shown in Figure 1. The tallest stem points to the right, the middle one to the left and the shortest one points forward.

Now place the first lily-of-the-valley stem at the back left hand and follow the line down with two other stems, each cut shorter (Fig. 2). The fourth lily-of-the-valley is cut even shorter and goes in front of the tallest.

At the right hand side, position the six rose buds as shown in Figure 3. Follow the photograph to fill the central area with fern leaves radiating from the centre. The large leaf overlaps the front rim of the dish. Now position the two gerberas to provide the focal point. Turn the arrangement around and use the final freesia and some foliage to fill in and finish off the back.

When using a clear glass dish you will find that marbles are useful for hiding the plasticine and also to give colour to the container.

Variations

Because the arrangement is based on groups of flowers you could easily change the colour of each type of flower. Soft pinks and white would blend admirably.

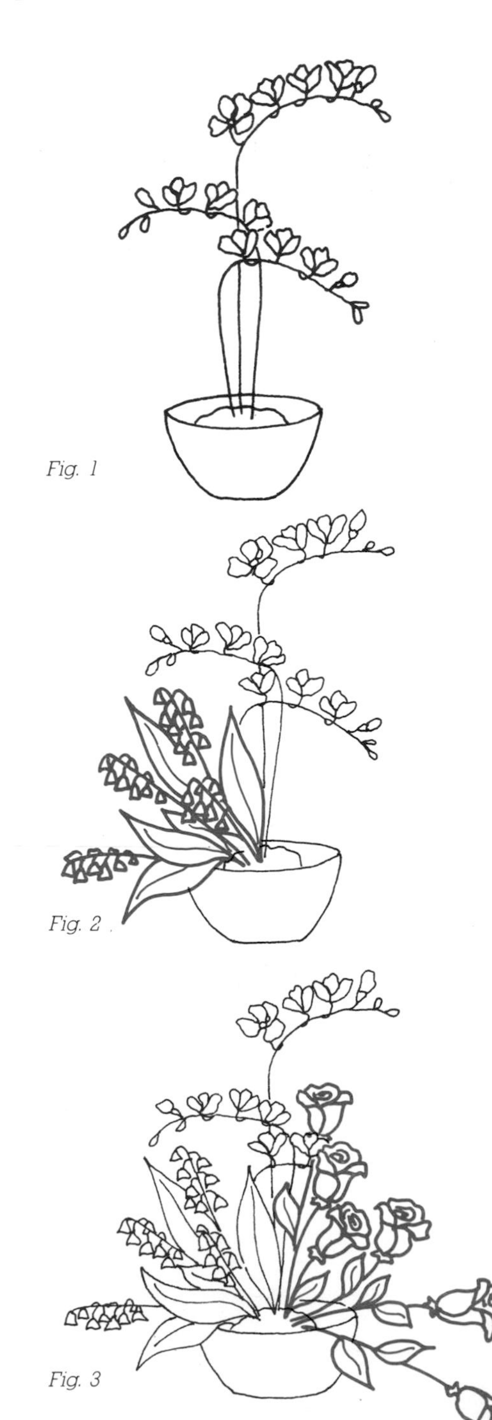

The items you will need

4 White freesias
4 White lily-of-the-valley
6 White rose buds
2 White gerbera
Fern foliage
Large begonia leaf
Glass dish, Marbles
Plasticine anchor, Oasis fix, Plasticine

Sweet Peas

The beauty of the sweet pea flower rarely mixes well with other blooms. This simple arrangement blends colours rather than outlines and soft pastel shades are the ones to choose.

How it is made

Fix a plasticine anchor in the centre of the dish with Oasis fix. Push a ball of plasticine onto the anchor.

Take six stems and cut through each stem just above the bottom flower so you have four flowers remaining (Fig. 1). Use these stems to circle the outer edge (Fig. 2) making sure contrasting colours are placed next to each other. These stems are pushed in and then bent downwards to a pleasing curve.

Use two stems of different colours but with five flowers remaining to make the central point of the arrangement.

The six single flower pieces are cut to leave a very short stem and then pushed around the main upright stems to cover the plasticine.

Cut six stems to leave three flowers per stem and position between the first six placements, around the edge (Fig. 3). Give each of these a curve to overlap the edge of the dish.

Use the rest of the stems to fill in and arrive at the final shape. Cut each of these remaining stems so that there is no more than three flowers to each of the stems.

Variations

Choosing one colour of sweet peas, possibly white or cream, and mixing these flowers with green foliage would provide an attractive alternative.

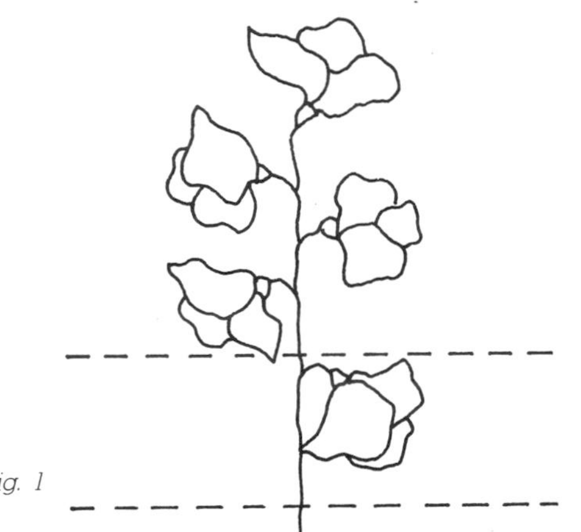

Fig. 1

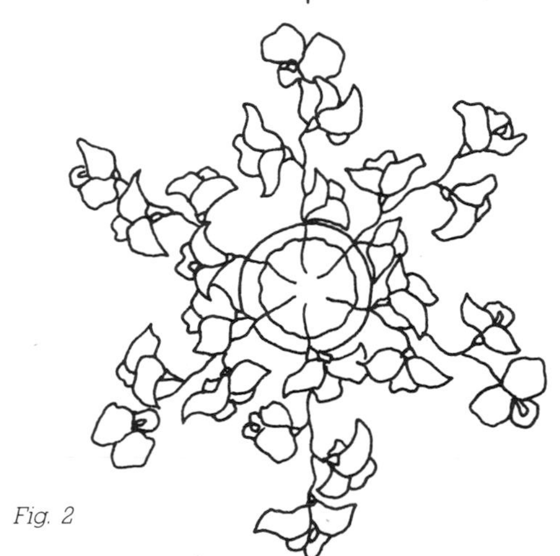

Fig. 2

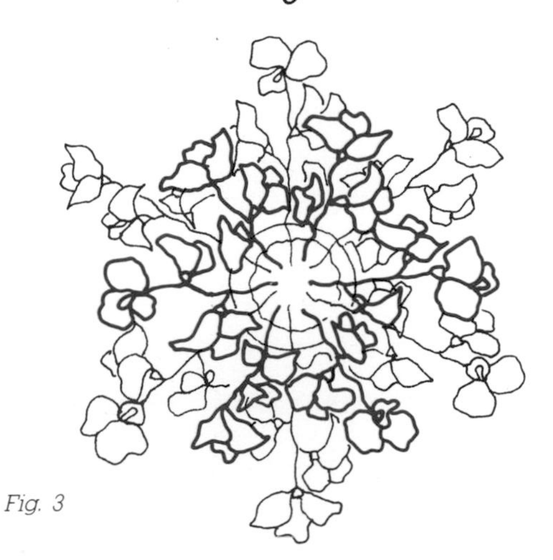

Fig. 3

The items you will need

21 Stems of sweet peas (5 flowers per stem)
Pedestal dish
Plasticine anchor, Oasis fix, plasticine

Pink Roses

As a symbol of beauty the rose is second to none – so it is worth taking some time to arrange the flowers. These seven perfect specimens would grace any bedroom or entrance hall.

How it is made

Wrap some plasticine in aluminium foil and push to the bottom of the vase. The use of the foil will keep the plasticine from sticking to the vase.

Cut the first rose to length so that the stem is approximately 1½ times the height of the vase. Position this rose slightly to the left of centre (Fig. 1). Now position the next two roses as shown in Figure 2. The bottom left rose is cut and positioned next so that the flower almost touches the rim of the vase.

Now complete the shape with the three central roses making sure each points in a slightly different direction.

The foliage which you have removed from the shorter stems is now made into individual pieces by adding a wire leg and covering the wire with stemwrap. Use these leaves to complete the outline of the arrangement and to break up any spaces between the roses.

Variations

This is more of an attractive vase of flowers rather than an arrangement, but it can be used as the basic shape for other blooms. You can use any flowers which are in season which you feel are in proportion to the vase you have in mind.

Fig. 1

Fig. 2

The items you will need

7 Pink roses
Vase
Plasticine
Aluminium foil

After Eight Candelabra

A formal dinner party can be transferred into a sumptuous occasion with the addition of a candelabra complete with an all-round arrangement which will be the centre of attention.

How it is made

Wrap plasticine in aluminium foil and press firmly into the candle cup. Make sure you have used enough plasticine to produce a level above the edge of the candle cup. Secure the candle cup in the centre part of the candelabra with Oasis fix – see page 17 for details.

Now fix the two candles in position, making sure they are truly vertical from all angles.

Start the arrangement with two stems of trailing ivy. Each is bent so that the leaves trail below the base of each of the orange candles (Fig. 1). The first three lily flowers are cut from a stem and positioned centrally in the candle cup so that the top bud is 1 inch (2.5cm) below the top of the candles (Fig. 2).

Now follow plan 3 to position the four main lily branches. These are all bent so that they are below the level of the candle cup.

The circle of marigolds are positioned just above the rim of the candle cup and the top part is finished with individual lily flowers cut from the other stem. Wire each one separately.

Now use any remaining foliage from the ivy or lily stems to fill in any gaps which you can find.

Make sure that you turn the arrangement around to check from all angles.

Variations

Matching candles with flower colour is important so take care. You could use different flowers, but see that they are in keeping with the expensive candelabra base.

The items you will need

4 Stems of orange lillies
(2 branches per stem)
4 Stems of white marigolds
(2 branches per stem)
4 Trailing ivy pieces
Silver candlestick for 3 candles
Candlestick cup
Plasticine, Oasis fix, aluminium foil

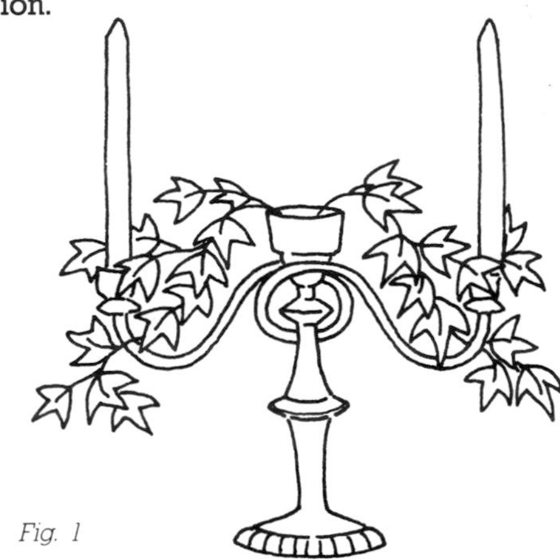

Fig. 1

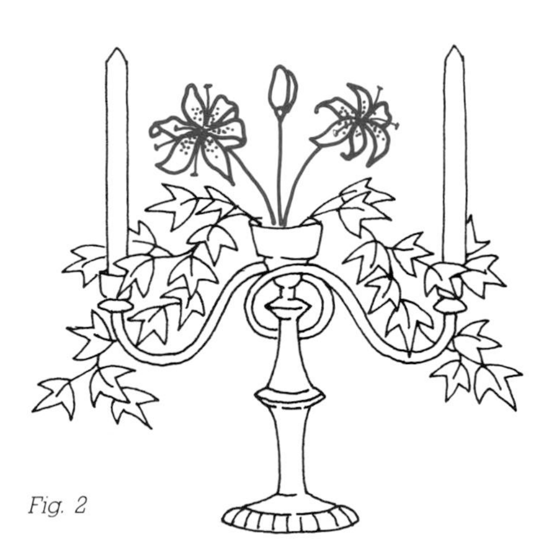

Fig. 2

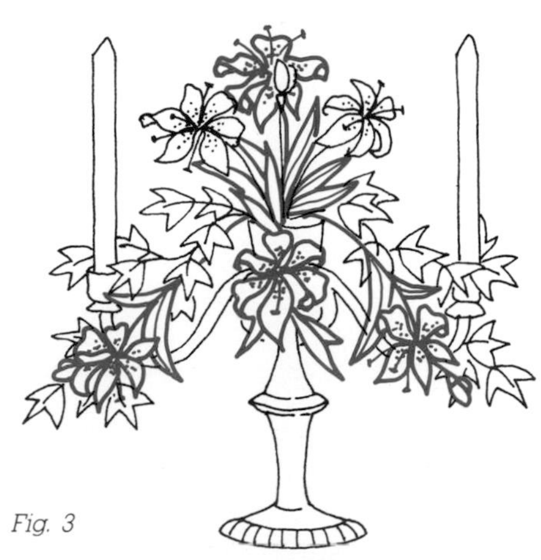

Fig. 3

Mauve Slice

The formal triangular shape of this arrangement looks attractive when complete with carnations of varying sizes and toning colours.

How it is made

Fix the plasticine anchor to the left hand side of the wood slice and push on a ball of plasticine.

The first stage is to make the three points of the triangle using the button carnations. Follow Figure 1 using a complete stem for the tall centre point, a stem cut down to seven flowers for the right hand point and a stem cut down to five flowers for the left hand point.

Now start from the top using the large pale carnations to create a pleasing shape within the triangular outline you have already created. Take care to get the length of each stem cut correctly and make sure each flower is pointing in a slightly different direction (Fig. 2).

Fill in between the carnations with the nine dianthus flowers. Cut each one and wire individually. These flowers should be recessed to give depth to the arrangement.

Turn the arrangement round and complete the back using any foliage or flowers to hide the mechanics and produce an attractive finish.

Variations

The shape can be equally appealing using a pedestal base and gives the arrangement a completely different look.

Fig. 1

Fig. 2

The items you will need

3 Stems of mauve button carnations
(14 blooms per stem)
3 Stems of mauve dianthus
(3 blooms per stem)
9 Large pale mauve carnations
Small woodslice
Plasticine anchor, Oasis fix, Plasticine

Greensleeves

Arrangements don't have to be full of flowers to have impact. As we show here the different types of foliage which are available can be used together to create a stunning effect which would grace any home.

How it is made

Firmly push a plasticine anchor into the bottom of the soapstone container using Oasis fix. Push on a ball of plasticine which should come up to the rim of the container.

The first placement is the central stem at the back. This should be approximately 1½ times the height of the container (Fig. 1). The next placements (Fig. 2) are the trailing pieces to the left and right hand sides. Try to use foliage which would naturally fall in this way – ivy is ideal.

Select at this stage the leaves which are to make the focal point of the arrangement and keep this to one side. Fill in the rest of the shape creating contrasts of colour and texutre as you go. All of the stems should radiate from the central point and none of this outer foliage should dominate.

Create the focal point in the centre and to the front of the container, making sure some of the leaves curl over the rim. Now turn the arrangement round and use any spare leaves to hide the mechanics and create a pleasing finish.

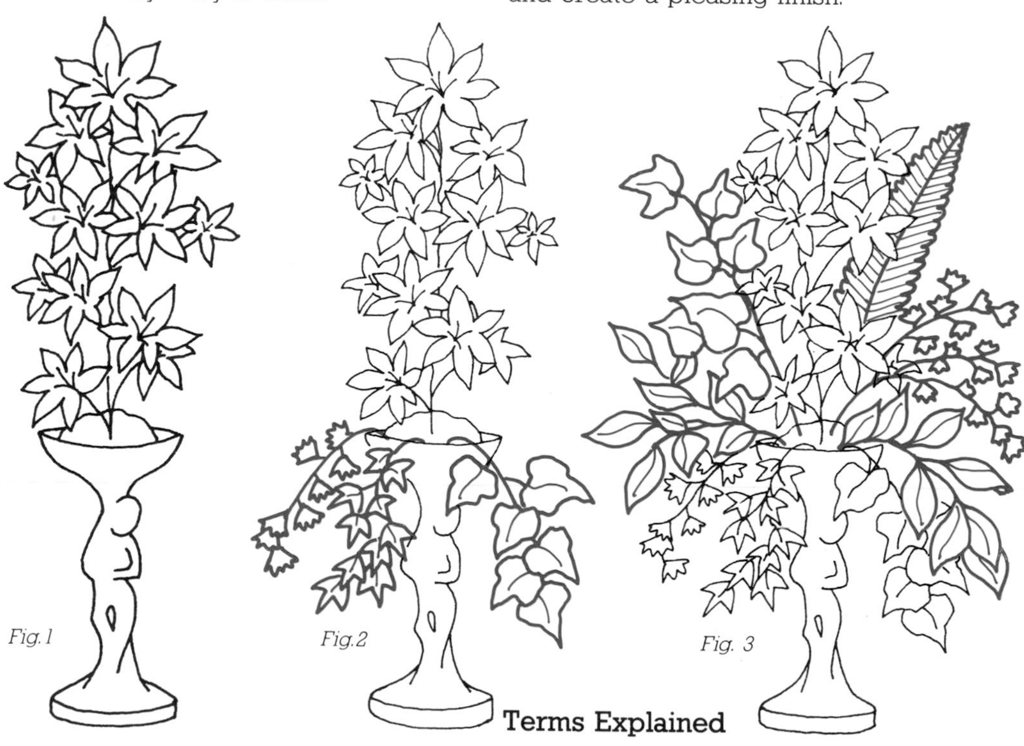

Fig. 1 *Fig. 2* *Fig. 3*

The items you will need

Try to obtain as many different kinds of foliage as possible. For example this arrangement contains three different types of ivy. Variegated leaves are important to add light and interest. So too is the contrasting shapes and textures of leaves. This is the sort of item which is useful in using up any foliage left over from other arrangements.

Terms Explained

Focal Point

This is the area to which the eye is naturally drawn and is often the main purpose of the arrangement. With this foliage work the eye goes to the central point because the stems radiate from there, but also because it is the area of greatest contrast and interest. With floral arrangements the largest bloom is often the natural focal point and should be positioned within the arrangement in a spot which is in keeping with the overall shape and the other flowers.

A COMPLETE STATE OF DEATH
John Gardner
IN THE HOUR BEFORE MIDNIGHT
Jack Higgins
THE SHROUD SOCIETY
Robert Crawford
I'M TRYING TO GIVE IT UP
Desmond Skirrow
ONCE IN A LIFETIME
James Mayo
DEATH OF THE WILD BIRD
John Newton Chance

Summer Splendour

A fireplace can be a dull focal point of a room during summer. However if you produce this vivacious arrangement you will add interest and colour which will last for years.

How it is made

Start by fixing a large piece of Dri-Hard to the base of the log basket using three plasticine anchors and Oasis fix. Now take a gladioli stem and position to the right hand side of the handle. Another gladioli is cut slightly shorter and placed just to the right of the first one. On the left one gladioli is used to form a base line and the other one is cut so that two more points are created (Fig. 1).

Use the stems of vine foliage to complete the triangular shape as shown in Figure 2, and then start to fill in with chrysanthemums and gerberas.

The four lemon roses are used in an inverted crescent line at the face of the arrangement (Fig. 3).

Recess some of the flowers to provide some depth, we have used pieces of forsythia. When the shape is full use the fern stems to radiate from the central points and to break any firm lines of the base.

Variations

There are various pieces of fireplace accessories which can be used as appropriate bases for this arrangement. Coal boxes, and buckets are suitable and so are wicker log baskets and trugs with low sides. You will need to adjust the proportions of the arrangement relative to the base you are using.

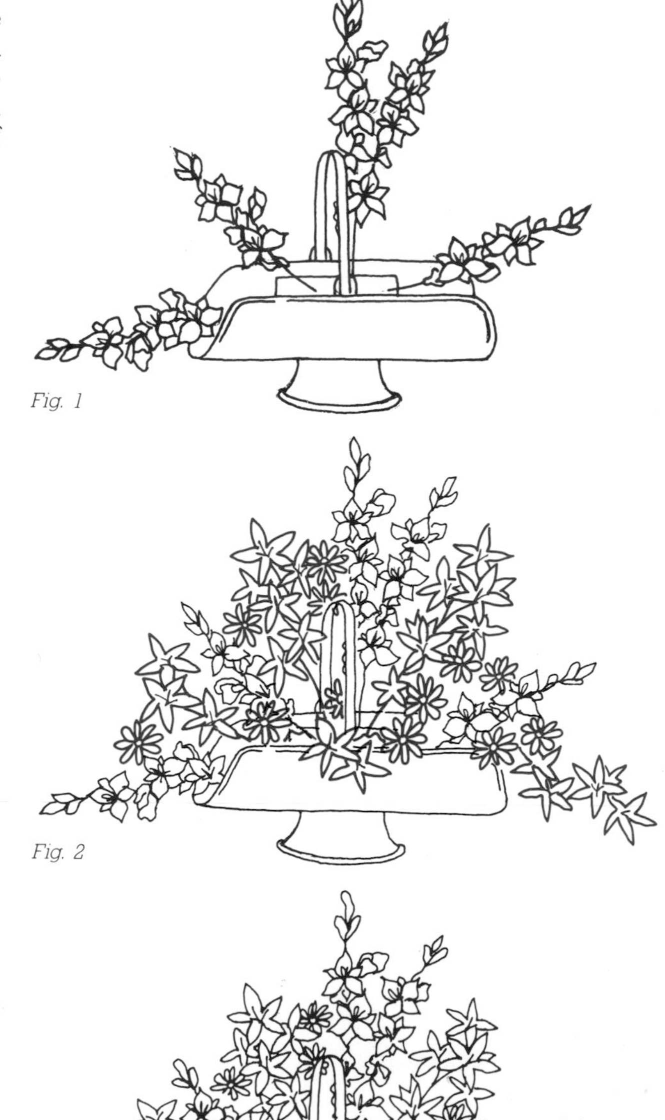

Fig. 1

Fig. 2

Fig. 3

The items you will need

4 Yellow roses
4 Orange gladioli
2 Stems of orange chrysanthemums (5 flowers per stem)
4 Yellow gerberas
3 Orange chrysanthemums
2 Stems of yellow forsythia (3 branches per stem)
3 Stems of yellow azalea
2 Stems of vine foliage (3 branches per stem)
12 Nephrolepis fern stems
1 Brass log basket
3 Plasticine anchors, Oasis fix, Dri-Hard

Lemon Candle

This white figurine candle holder makes a beautiful base for an attractive table centre of lemon and white silk flowers.

How it is made

Cut the lemon candle to length and fix in the topmost candle holder. If the base of the candle is too small to fit snugly, simply wrap Oasis fix around the bottom of the candle. In the lower holder fit a candle cup using Oasis fix. Inside the candle cup goes a plasticine anchor stuck to the centre base of the candle cup with Oasis fix. Push onto the anchor a ball of Dri-Hard which has been covered in aluminium foil.

Start the arrangement by cutting the daisy flower stems to length and positioning to make a circular outline, as shown in Figure 1. Now cut the rose bud stems to different lengths and position to mix in with daisies but retain this circular theme (Fig. 2). Use nine of the buds at the front and keep the other three to finish off the back of the arrangement.

Fill in the front with daisy flowers keeping some space between each flower if possible. Avoid overcrowding at this stage.

The arrangement is completed with single-loop bows of ribbon. Use four or five in the front and one at the back. Fill in the back with remaining roses and daisy flowers.

Fig. 1

Variations

Using one colour of candle, flowers and ribbon it is possible to make scores of different arrangements. Your only limitation will be the availability of small flower heads which are essential for this dainty and long-lived decoration.

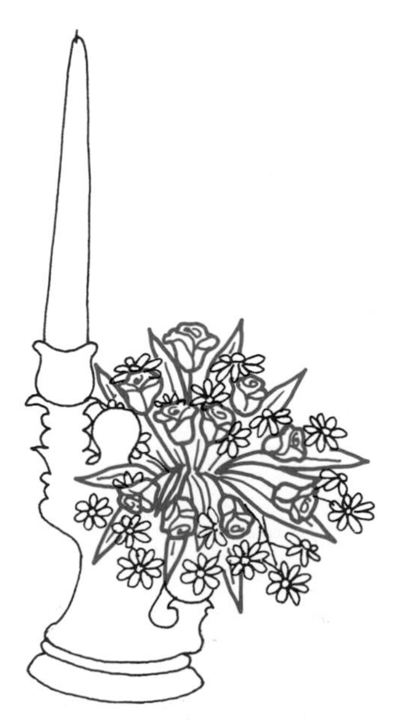

Fig. 2

The items you will need

12 Lemon and white rose buds
12 Stems yellow daisy flowers
2 Yards narrow lemon ribbon
1 Lemon candle
1 White candle cup
1 White figurine candle holder
Plasticine anchor, Oasis fix, Dri-Hard
Aluminium foil

Childs Play

Even children can be encouraged to create arrangements especially if they are based on a garden theme. This one was completed by two boys aged 9 and 10.

How it is made

Creating the tree from a stem of pussy willow is probably the only help your children will need to re-create this arrangement. Start by bending the branches to a weeping shape and then cut the stem to length.

Press a ball of Dri-Hard around the bottom of the stem and make a flat base so that the tree stands upright (Fig. 1). Leave to set for at least 12 hours.

Take a round tray and three large stones to create different levels and position the tree to the back of the tray (Fig. 2).

Fill in with soil and top off the surface with moss. After positioning the figures create different flower beds with small silk blooms. With this arrangement the smaller the flowers the better will be the effect, but if your children are intent on creating the garden let them choose the blooms which appeal to them. The final result may be a little garish, but changes can always be encouraged at a later date.

To keep the moss in good condition mist the surface with plain water occasionally.

Fig. 2

Variations

The tree can be created with any fine leaved foliage or you can use a twig and glue flowers or leaves to the stem. Any flowers which are in proportion to the overall size will be acceptable.

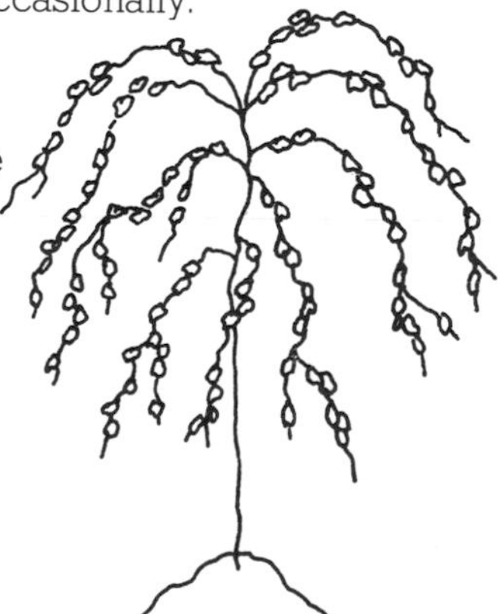

Fig. 1

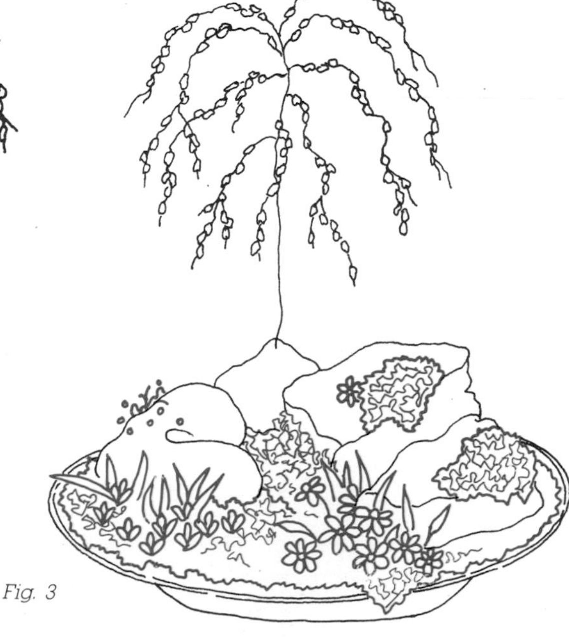

Fig. 3

The items you will need

1 Stem of pussy willow
Rocks
Various small flowers
Moss
Figures
Tray, Dri-Hard

Carnation Centrepiece

This all-round arrangement makes a great decoration for winter tea times. It is small enough not to be intrusive yet striking enough to get some appreciative attention.

How it is made

Push a ball of plasticine into the top of the candlestick so that there is sufficient material above the top to take all the flower stems.

Prepare the candle with cocktail sticks (see page 17) and position centrally and vertically.

Start with four spikes of pink flowers and position equally around the candlestick. Bend the stems so that the stems point downwards (Fig. 1). Between each of these spikes position a carnation (Fig. 2). Above the original spikes position four more carnations (Fig. 3).

Around the base of the candle position pieces of light pink flowers and pink blossom. Just outside this circle position four carnations with short stems close to the plasticine. In between these flowers position pink blossom to fill in any gaps.

Make leaf bows from the four pieces of foliage (see page 60) and place close to the candle.

Finish off with short spikes of broom foliage to add points of interest all around the arrangement.

Variations

Carnations are available in many different colours and as long as you can match the colour of your choice with a candle any hue would be attractive.

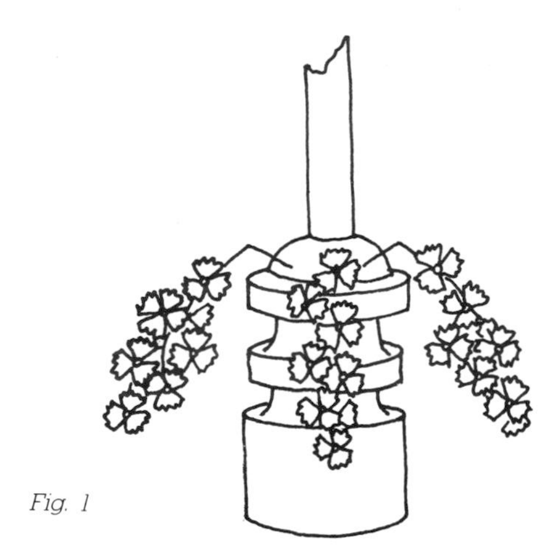

Fig. 1

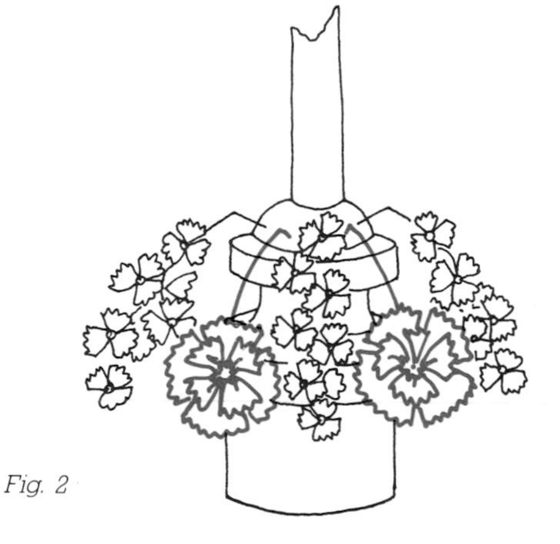

Fig. 2

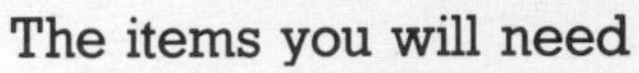

The items you will need

12 Red carnations
4 Stems of pink blossom
1 Stem of white broom
1 Spray of dark pink flowers
1 Spray of light pink flowers
4 Narrow green leaves
1 Ruby red candle
Wooden candlestick
Cocktail sticks, Plasticine

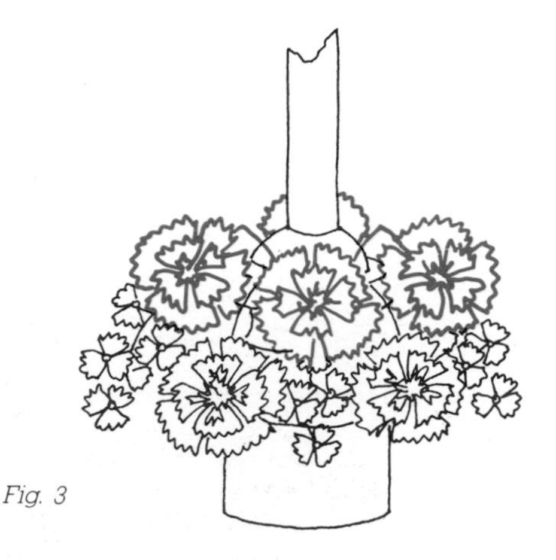

Fig. 3

Copper Cocktail

The colours and shape of this arrangement were selected to go in front of this attractive Johnnie Walker tray. Even without it, the dish of flowers would be impressive, especially in an alcove.

How it is made

Fix a plasticine anchor to the left of centre in the bottom of the dish and push a ball of plasticine onto it. Prop up the tray behind the dish so that you know the shape and size you have to follow.

The first stem of three roses goes to the back left and is the tallest point. The right hand point of the crescent is a rose stem with two flowers and the left hand point a single rose (Fig. 1).

Place the first three dahlias as shown in Figure 2 and then complete the outline of the crescent with five rose flowers.

Complete the centre placements with three more dahlias and then recess a few roses to give depth to the arrangement.

To complete the picture use any material left over to finish off the back of the arrangement.

Fig. 1

Fig. 2

Variations

Choose your flowers to match the colour of the back piece. A simple Delft dish in blue and white could easily be matched with flowers of the same colour. Avoid circular plates which can be a difficult shape to mirror in the arrangement.

The items you will need
7 Stems of brown roses (3 flowers per stem)
9 Beige dahlias (peony-flowered type)
Brown dish, Tray
Plasticine anchor, Oasis fix, Plasticine

Waterside Blossoms

The arching branches of springtime blossoms is contrasted by a profusion of sun-seeking azaleas in this arrangement which sits happily on a circular marble base.

How it is made

Fix a plasticine anchor to the centre of the small white saucer and push a ball of Dri-Hard onto the anchor.

Start by bending the branches of mauve blossom into shape. The first stem is shown in Figure 1 and the second in Figure 2. This will provide the outline which is to be filled with lemon blooms.

The azalea blooms we used did not have flexible wire stems, so it was necessary to wire each stem. If you need to do the same, simply use the technique for wiring a branch as shown on page 15. Make sure all the metal wire is covered with stemwrap.

Position the stones which will hide the saucer and then start to fill in with azalea blooms. Some of the blooms should overlap the stones so that the grouping made is a single visual whole. To complete the arrangement, recess a few flowers close to the mechanics so that the base is hidden.

Variations

The blossom branches in lemon or white could be contrasted with any flower of soft hues. Lilies or iris are available in various colours and they could be used with great effect.

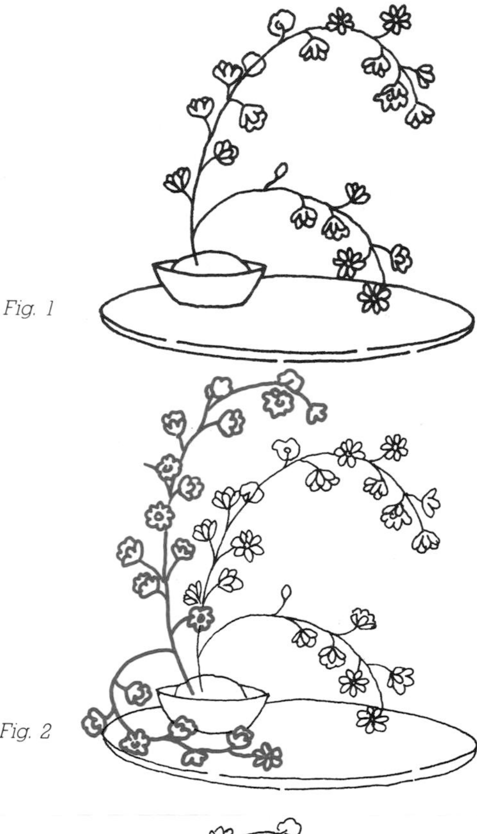

Fig. 1

Fig. 2

Fig. 3

The items you will need

2 Stems of mauve blossom
2 Stems of lemon azaleas
(7 blooms per stem)
Stones, Marble base
White saucer
Plasticine anchor, Oasis fix, Dri-Hard

Orange Glow

This all-round arrangement with candle would make a warm and attractive centrepiece for an early spring dinner table.

How it is made

Firmly fix the anchor in the centre of the round dish and push on a ball of plasticine.

Prepare the candle by taping cocktail sticks to its base (page 17) and position centrally and vertically in the plasticine.

Start with four stems of narcissus which form the oval shape at the four points of the compass. Between each of these flowers position one stem of orange blooms which should be just inside the oval outline (Fig. 1).

Now take the four chrysanthemum blooms and cut to length so that they point outwards just above the stems of the narcissus (Fig. 2).

Place four of the stems of orange and gold flowers around the candle alternating their colours to add interest.

Fill in with narcissus and gold and orange flowers to maintain a cushion of colour which is low and interesting. A few individual blooms recessed close to the plasticine will add depth.

Variations

Chrysanthemums are available in a host of colours and pale lemon would look attractive with the same orange and gold flowers.

Fig. 1

Fig. 2

The items you will need

6 Stems of orange flowers
6 Stems of gold flowers
12 Stems of white narcissus
4 Cream chrysanthemums
1 Candle
1 White dish
Plasticine anchor, Oasis fix, Plasticine

Finishing Off

To complete any arrangement it is always worth while viewing it from all angles to check that there are no unsightly sides. Here is an arrangement which at the back reveals all the mechanics of stems and base materials. It will pay dividends if this is disguised so that the arrangement can be viewed from any angle.

Find some foliage, odd flowers or some spare ribbon and add wire stems to each. Covering the wires with stem-wrap will improve the appearance. Start by using three pieces of foliage with longish stems to make a triangle.

Continue to fill in at the base, working towards the centre. Finish off with a flower or two. On the right you can see the back of the completed arrangement. When finished off in this manner the decoration can be placed in any position.

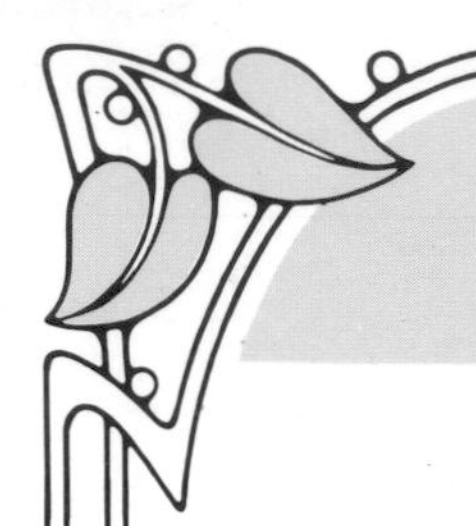

Index

Accessories 13
After Eight Candelabra 72
Alabaster Smoothness 66
Anchor 6
Apricot and Cream 24
Asymmetrical triangle 20
Azalea 32,64,80,90

Bases 8
Basket of Blue 54
Baskets 8,54
Blossom Tree 78
Bowl of Plants 48
Bromeliad 34
Bulrushes 60

Candle 16,82,86
Candle cup 9,17,72,82
Candle holders 17
Candlestick 9,72,86
Carnation Centrepiece 86
Carnations 32,38,40,42,54,74,86
Chelsea Boot 50
Child's Play 84
Chrysanthemum 38,80,92
Circular arrangement 21
Containers 9
Cocktail sticks 17
Copper Cocktail 88
Cornflower 54
Crescent arrangement 21
Cyclamen 48

Daffodil 46
Daisy 26,36,58,64,82
Daisy Basket 58
Dahlia 88
Days of Spring 46
Delphinium 24,54
Dianthus 74
Double leg wire 14,15
Dracaena 48
Dri-Hard 7

Equipment 6
Euonymus 48

Fern 50,80
Figure of eight bow 19
Finishing off 94
Fittonia 34,62
Flowers 10
Flower wiring 14
Foam bases 7
Forsythia 80
Foliage 12,76
Freesia 42,52,66
Fuchsia 56

Gardenia 62
Gardenia Cage 62
Gerbera 38,66,80
Gladiolus 40,80
Golden Lightness 64
Greensleeves 76

Handful of Freesias 52
Hogarth curve shape 21,26
Horizontal arrangement 21
Houseplants 34,48
Hyacinth 26

Iris & Pussy Willow 28
Iris 28,42,46
Ivy 28,34,44,48,62,72

Knife 6

L-shape arrangement 20
Lazy-S shape 21,26
Leaf loops 28,42,60
Leaf wiring 14
Lemon Candle 82
Lily flowers 40,72
Lily-of-the-valley 38,54,66
Lotus Eaters 22

Marigolds 72
Mauve slice 74
Mechanics 6
Moss 46,84

Narcissus 92

Oasis fix 6,17
Oasis foam 6
Oasis tape 6
Orange Glow 92
Oval arrangement 21

Peach delight 30
Pink Roses 70
Pink Crescent 36
Pink Sensation 40
Plastic foam 6
Plasticine 6
Plasticine anchors 6
Poppy Fields 44
Poppy 44
Pussy Willow 28,84

Ribbons 18,64,82
Ribbon tying 18,19
Riverside Tulips 60
Roses 24,26,30,32,50,58,64,66,70,82,88
Ruby Woodslice 32

Saintpaulia 34,48
Sansevieria 48
Saucers 9
Scissors 6
Scroll base 8
Shapes 20,21
Silk curves 26
Single loop ribbon 18
Snowdrop 46
Spring Profusion 42
Stay soft 6
Stem binding tape 6
Stem wiring 15
Stub wires 6
Summer Splendour 80
Summer Sun 38
Symmetrical triangle 20,24

Table centre 38,40
Tail ribbon 18
Tradescantia 34
Trails of Fuchsia 56
Triple loop ribbon 19
Tropical Dish 34
Tulips 60

Vertical arrangement 20
Vine foliage 80

Waterside Blossoms 90
Wicker baskets 8
Willow 46
Wire 6
Wire cutters 6
Wiring 14,15
Woodslice 8,32,74
Wrought iron containers 9,21,30,62,64

Zinnia 36